U.S. ARMY COMBAT STRESS CONTROL
HANDBOOK

DEPARTMENT OF THE ARMY

THE LYONS PRESS

Guilford, Connecticut
An imprint of The Globe Pequot Press

The Lyons Press is an imprint of The Globe Pequot Press

10 9 8 7 6 5 4 3 2 1

Printed in The United States of America

Designed by Claire Zoghb

ISBN 1-58574-783-1

Library of Congress Cataloging-in-Publication Data is available on file.

CONTENTS

PREFACE

This field manual (FM) provides information for all leaders and staff on the control of combat stressors and the prevention of stress casualties. It identifies the leaders' responsibilities for controlling stress and recognizing the effects of stress on their personnel. It reviews Army operational doctrine for war and operations other than war. It identifies likely stressors and recommends actions for leaders to implement for the prevention and management of stress. The manual describes the positive and negative combat stress behavior associated with stress and provides leader actions to minimize battle fatigue risk factors. It provides the many different military branches and disciplines with a common conceptual framework, knowledge base, and vocabulary so they work together toward controlling stress. It provides information on how stressors and the stress process interact to improve or disrupt military performance. It identifies the supporting role of special staffs such as the chaplain and the Judge Advocate General. This manual also identifies the responsibilities of medical personnel for prevention, treatment, and management of battle fatigue and stress-related casualties.

The proponent of this publication is the United States (US) Army Medical Department Center and School (AMEDDC&S). Send comments and recommendations on Department of the Army (DA) Form 2028 directly to Commander, AMEDDC&S, ATTN: HSMC-FCD, Fort Sam Houston, Texas 78234-6123.

Unless this publication states otherwise, masculine nouns and pronouns do not refer exclusively to men.

The use of trade names in this publication does not imply endorsement by the US Army, but is intended only to assist in the identification of a specific product.

U.S. ARMY
COMBAT
STRESS
CONTROL
HANDBOOK
—

CHAPTER 1

OVERVIEW OF COMBAT STRESS CONTROL

1-1. INTRODUCTION

This chapter presents the concept and scope of combat stress control. It reviews historical experiences with stress casualties in different intensities of conflict and looks at the potential stressors in high-tech battles. It lists the responsibilities for combat stress control of all junior (direct) and senior (organizational) leaders, staffs, chaplains, and health care providers. It also discusses the responsibilities of specialized combat stress control/mental health personnel.

Note: Battle fatigue and misconduct stress behaviors are preventable with strong effective leadership.

1-2. COMBAT STRESS CONTROL

a.   Controlling combat stress is often the deciding factor—the difference between victory and defeat—in all forms of human conflict. Stressors are a fact of combat and soldiers must face them. It is controlled combat stress (when properly focused by training, unit cohesion, and leadership) that gives soldiers the necessary alertness, strength, and endurance to accomplish their mission. Controlled combat stress can call forth stress reactions of loyalty, selflessness, and heroism. Conversely, uncontrolled combat stress causes erratic or harmful behavior that disrupts or interferes with accomplishment of the unit mission. Uncontrolled combat stress could impair mission performance and may bring disgrace, disaster, and defeat.

b.   The art of war aims to impose so much stress on the enemy soldiers that they lose their will to fight. Both sides try to do this and at times accept severe stress themselves in order to inflict greater stress on the enemy. To win, combat stress must be controlled.

c.   The word *control* has been chosen deliberately to focus thinking and action within the Army. Since the same word may have contrasting connotations to different people, it is important to make its intended meaning clear. The word *control* is used (rather than the word *management*) to emphasize the active steps which leaders, supporting personnel, and individual soldiers must take to keep stress within the acceptable range. This does not mean that control and management are mutually exclusive terms. Management is, by definition, the exercise of control. Within common usage, however, and especially within Army usage, management has the connotation of being a somewhat detached, number-driven, higher echelon process rather than a direct, inspirational, leadership process.

d.   Stress is the body's and mind's process for dealing with uncertain change and danger. Elimination of stress is both impossible and undesirable in either the Army's combat or peacetime missions.

e.   The objectives of stress control are as follows:

(1) To keep stress within acceptable limits for mission performance and to achieve the ideal (optimal) level of stress when feasible.

(2) To return stress to acceptable limits when it becomes temporarily disruptive.

(3) To progressively increase tolerance to stress so that soldiers can endure and function under the extreme stress which is unavoidable in combat.

f.   How can stress be controlled? Stress is controlled in the same ways other complex processes are controlled.

(1) Monitor the signs of stress and recognize when and if they change. To be effective, this recognition should come well before the stress becomes disruptive and causes dysfunction.

(2) Identify and monitor the causes of stress; that is, the stressors. Stress and stressors are defined in Chapter 2.

(3) Classify the stressors into those which can be controlled

(increased, decreased, avoided, or otherwise changed) versus those which cannot be controlled.

(4) Control those stressors which can be changed by focusing the stress in the desired direction, either up or down.

(5) Help soldiers adapt to the stressors which cannot be changed.

(6) Learn (and teach) how to directly lower (or raise) the stress level within the individual soldier as needed, at specific times, in specific situations.

1-3. SCOPE OF COMBAT STRESS CONTROL

Combat stress control is much more than just a few stress reduction techniques which busy leaders are supposed to learn from books or mental health workers and use now and then when the stress seems intense. Army combat stress control activities must be a part of every-thing the Army does. Combat stress control must be a natural part of the three continuums of Army life: *responsibility, location,* and *Army mission.* Note that a weakness or gap anywhere in these three contin-uums can cause weakness, overloads, or breakdowns in other aspects of Army life.

a. *Responsibility.* Responsibility for combat stress control re-quires a continuous interaction that begins with every soldier and his buddies. It also involves the soldier's family members. The interaction continues through the small team's combat lifesaver (when there is one) and the combat medic. Stress control requires special involve-ment from direct (small unit) leaders. The responsibility extends up through the organizational leaders and their staffs (both officers and noncommissioned officers [NCOs]) at all echelons. Appendix A de-scribes combat stress risk factors and prescribes leaders' actions to control them. Leaders, staffs, and individual soldiers all receive assis-tance from the supporting chaplains, the medical personnel, and combat stress control/mental health personnel (see Appendix B for information pertaining to combat stress control units). If any link in the chain of responsibility is weak, it is the responsibility of the other members of the chain to strengthen it.

    b.   *Location.* The location for combat stress control extends continuously—

- From the site of battle, disaster, or rigorous duty.
- Through the unit's forward and rearward support areas.
- Through the communications zone (COMMZ), if present.
- To the continental United States (CONUS).
- To the unit's home station.
- To the rear detachment.
- To the family support group.
- To the Army hospitals and medical centers.

The location even extends to the Department of Veterans Affairs and veterans organizations after the soldiers' discharge, medical separation, or retirement. Preventive efforts, and also treatment for stress dysfunction, should be actively accomplished at each location. If stress control is weak at any one location, this can cause stress and breakdown not only there, but elsewhere in other locations.

    c.   *Army Missions.* The Army operations that require combat stress control are all-inclusive. They extend continuously—

- From garrison maintenance activities.
- To peacetime training exercises.
- To operations other than war.
- To war.
- To the integrated battlefield.

The same basic stress control principles apply across the entire range of Army operations. Within our rapidly changing world, many Army units have had their missions shift across a wide range of operations in a matter of weeks, sometimes with little advance warning. Individual soldiers, family members, unit leaders and staffs, chaplains, and medics (including the mental health/combat stress control teams) must be involved and work together continuously. They must practice stress control against the frequent minor stressors and the occasional severe stressors of peacetime. This, and only this, enables them to be ready on short notice for the extreme stressors of war.

1-4. HISTORICAL EXPERIENCE

    a.   *Origins of the Combat Stress Control Concept.*

    (1) Combat stress control is not new. The basic leadership techniques which this manual will review were discovered and taught by successful military leaders through the centuries and have long been cornerstones of US Army leadership training. Combat stress control medical doctrine for preventing and treating stress casualties is sometimes mistakenly said to have originated from the Israeli Defense Force experiences in the 1970s and 1980s. Quite the contrary, the US Army learned that basic doctrine from its allies during World War I (WWI).

    (a) The French and British discovered that if stress casualties were evacuated far to the rear, many became chronic psychiatric cripples. If treated quickly close to their units, most recovered and returned to duty. The US Army Surgeon General of that time recommended that we adopt a three-echelon system for prevention, triage, treatment, and return to duty of stress casualties.

    1. *First echelon.* The US Army attached a trained psychiatrist to each division. The psychiatrist's role was to advise command in the prevention of stress casualties, to screen out the unsuitable, and to assure that overstressed soldiers were rested and returned to duty within the division whenever possible. Following British practice, stress casualties in the division were labeled "Not Yet Diagnosed, Nervous" (NYDN). This avoided even the suggestion of physical injury implied by the dramatic popular label "shell shock" or the implication of psychiatric illness conveyed by the official diagnosis of "war neurosis." Under good conditions, 70 percent of stress casualties were returned to duty within the division.

    2. *Second echelon.* Behind the divisions in WWI, the US Army had specialized neurological hospitals (150 beds) whose sole function was to provide additional brief rest and rehabilitation to those NYDN cases whom the division psychiatrist was unable to return to duty. These neuropsychiatric facilities also provided brief rest and rehabilitation to persistent cases of "gas mania" or "gas hysteria" who believed they had suffered chemical injuries, even though they

had not been truly injured. About 55 percent of the cases sent to these facilities returned to duty in an average of two weeks.

3. *Third echelon.* Further to the rear was a specialized base hospital which provided several weeks of additional treatment for cases who failed to improve in the neurological hospital. It returned many of those cases to useful duty.

(b) The three-echelon system worked well, but on occasion when the tactical situation interfered with forward treatment, it clearly showed the superiority of the forward-deployed part of the program.

(2) The experience of WWI was forgotten between wars. It had to be rediscovered in World War II (WWII) after several disastrous experiences when large numbers of psychiatric casualties were overevacuated in the early battles. By late WWII in the European and Mediterranean theaters, all divisions again had a division psychiatrist with mental health assistants. The psychiatrist supervised a Training and Rehabilitation Center in the division rear. The psychiatrists trained and supervised the regimental and battalion surgeons in recognizing and treating combat exhaustion or battle fatigue cases. Most regimental combat teams (equivalent to our brigades) had an exhaustion center in the regimental trains area. Many battalions maintained a rest area at the battalion field kitchens. The surgeons supervised these facilities to assure that soldiers who were rotated back to them recovered quickly and returned to duty. Behind the division there were specialized clearing companies commanded and staffed by psychiatrists. These clearing companies provided additional treatment for nonresponders or problem cases. Specialized base hospitals were located in the COMMZ.

(3) Following WWII, the lessons learned were embodied in a table of organization and equipment (TOE) unit, the mobile psychiatric detachment, or "KO" team. These teams functioned very effectively in Korea.

b. *Experience in War.*

(1) In the WWII Mediterranean and European theaters, the average incidence of combat exhaustion casualties was one case requiring medical holding and treatment for every four wounded in

action (WIA) (a 1:4 ratio). In really intense or prolonged fighting, the ratio rose to 1:2. On the Gothic line in Italy, the 1st Armored Division suffered 137 combat exhaustion casualties for 250 WIA (a 1:1.8 ratio). Overall, with the correct treatment, 50 to 70 percent of combat exhaustion casualties returned to combat within 3 days, and most of the remainder returned to useful duty within a few weeks.

(2) During WWII the 6th Marine Division was involved in the Battle of Okinawa. They fought day after day and were up against a determined, dug-in Japanese resistance, rain and mud, and heavy artillery. The division suffered 2,662 WIA and had 1,289 combat exhaustion casualties (a ratio to WIA of 1:2). Many of the combat exhaustion cases were evacuated to Navy ships offshore and few of those cases ever returned to duty.

(3) In the Pacific theater in WWII, there was about one neuropsychiatric casualty evacuated from the theater for every one WIA (a 1:1 ratio). Many of these troops appeared psychotic (bizarrely out of touch with reality). Most of these, however, did not come from the combat units or areas. They were combat service support (CSS) troops left behind by the war on the hot jungle or coral islands or the cold, damp Aleutian Islands. The stressors were the combination of isolation, monotony, boredom, chronic discomfort, and low-grade illness from the environment, plus fear of disease, injury, and surprise attack. In retrospect, it was realized that evacuating these bizarre stress reaction cases home only encouraged more soldiers to "go crazy" when they temporarily reached their limit of tolerance to stress. It would have been better to have sent them to rest camps close to their units. This might have returned the majority quickly to duty, as was done with the combat exhaustion cases in the European and Mediterranean theaters.

(4) It was also shown in WWII that tough training and esprit de corps prevented many battle fatigue casualties. Elite units, such as the ranger and airborne units, had less than one battle fatigue casualty for every ten WIA. This unit cohesiveness prevailed even in combat assaults, such as Normandy and Arnhem, where extremely high casualties were suffered. Unit cohesiveness also prevailed during prolonged fighting like the Battle of the Bulge.

(5) During the Yom Kippur War (1973), the Israeli experience confirmed the risk of stress casualties in the modern, high-tech, continuous operations (CONOPS) battle. The Israelis counted on the high cohesion and training of their troops and leaders to keep stress casualties to a minimum. They were caught, however, by strategic and tactical surprise and were forced to mobilize on a religious (fasting) holiday. They sent their reserves piecemeal into battle. Their Arab opponents, whom they had previously discounted as inefficient, used massed artillery, armor, and wire-guided missiles. The Arab units followed the Soviet CONOPS, echeloned-attack doctrine. Israeli estimates of stress casualties suggest that large numbers of Israeli soldiers, including veterans and leaders, became unable to function solely because of stress. Stress casualties were frequent in the Golan Heights fighting, in the initial defense of the Sinai, and during the recrossing of the Suez Canal. Since the Israeli Defense Force had no plans for treatment and return to duty, all such cases were evacuated to hospitals in Israel. True to the experience of WWI and WWII, many of these Israeli soldiers who were evacuated remain psychiatrically disabled today.

(6) After the 1973 war, the Israelis instituted a model program of leadership training and medical/mental health support. This was intended to prevent combat stress casualties and to treat those cases which occurred in the brigade and division support areas. However, in the 1982 Lebanon invasion, many cases were inadvertently evacuated by helicopter to Israel in the initial haste of the invasion. Few of these cases returned to full duty, while 60 to 80 percent of those treated in Lebanon did.

(7) One Israeli armored battalion trapped in a desperate night action against the Syrians had approximately 30 combat stress cases and 30 WIA (a 1:1 ratio). A combat engineer battalion which was accidentally bombed by an Israeli fighter-bomber had approximately 25 killed in action (KIA) and 200 WIA. This same battalion soon had 20 immediate combat stress casualties. Approximately 25 other soldiers developed delayed stress reactions over succeeding days (a ratio to WIA of 1:4.4). Even the Israelis' strong preventive program could not completely prevent battle fatigue casualties in a high-tech war.

c. *Experience in Vietnam.*

(1) In Vietnam, battle fatigue casualty rates rarely exceeded one per ten WIA. The reasons for the few battle fatigue casualties included the sporadic nature of fighting and our air and artillery superiority. Other factors were well-supplied fire bases, scheduled rest and recuperation (R&R), and a fixed combat tour. All these factors kept most battle fatigue cases at levels which could be treated in their units and did not require medical holding or hospitalization.

(2) Other behavioral problems related to loneliness and frustration, however, were associated with combat stress in Vietnam. Serious incidents of poor discipline occurred, including commission of atrocities at My Lai (March 1968), combat refusal, and even "fragging" (murder) of leaders. These events threatened unit cohesion and the chain of command. By 1970–1971, when US ground forces were rarely committed to offensive operations, "neuropsychiatric casualties," especially drug and alcohol abuse and addiction, became epidemic. By September 1971, neuropsychiatric cases accounted for over 60 percent of all medical evacuations from the theater. Today those misconduct problems are recognized as having contributed to the high incidence of delayed post-traumatic stress disorder (PTSD) in Vietnam veterans. Due to the different nature of the stress, these types of misconduct stress behaviors are more likely than battle fatigue in operations other than war (conflict). These misconduct stress behaviors can seriously undermine the objectives and successes of the mission.

d. *Experience in Catastrophic Events During Peacetime and Operations Other Than War.* Within the past few years, numerous accidents and hostile incidents have demonstrated the value of crisis stress control for soldiers, their families, and civilians caught in the turmoil of peacetime operations. Some recent historical events are listed in Table 1-1. Unit leaders aided by post and hospital mental health personnel, chaplains, and others played key roles in providing crisis stress control for many of these tragic incidents. In the peacetime military, as in civilian police, fire, and disaster relief, stress debriefing of critical incidents has proved its value in preventing and treating disabling PTSD.

1-5. EFFECTS OF BATTLE ON SOLDIERS, UNITS, AND LEADERS

a.   War is fundamentally a contest of wills fought by men, not machines. Ardant Du Picq, a 19th century French officer and student of men in battle, reminded us that, "You can reach into the well of courage only so many times before the well runs dry." Even before that, Marshall De Saxe, writing in the 18th century pointed out that, "A soldier's courage must be reborn daily," and went on to say that the most important task of leaders was to understand this, to care for and prepare soldiers before battle, and to use tactics during battle which recognize that courage must be renewed.

b.   Commanders must understand that in battle men and units are more likely to fail catastrophically than gradually. Commanders and staffs, assisted by combat stress control personnel, medics, chaplains, and others, must be alert to subtle indicators of fatigue, fear, poor discipline, and reduced morale. They must take measures to deal with these symptoms before their cumulative effects cause a unit to collapse. Staffs and commanders at higher levels must be advised about the impact of intense or prolonged combat on subordinate units. Military organizations can fight at peak efficiency for only so long. Prolonged demands of combat cause efficiency to drop even when physical losses are not great.

c.   A unit may not be capable of performing its mission adequately if soldier resources are depleted because—

- Vigilance deteriorates.
- Determinations and calculations become inaccurate.
- Reports become faulty.
- Decisions become slow and inaccurate.
- Orders are misunderstood/forgotten.
- Weapons are misused/underused.
- Maintenance and preplanning are forgotten.
- Motivation to perform duties decreases.
- Leaders' effectiveness decreases.
- Training becomes ineffective.

d.   Degradation of soldiers' performance means that they lose a portion of their normal effectiveness. Continuous, unrelieved operations and excessive stress degrade performance and erode soldier resources. Combat capability is cut whether the unit is at 50 percent strength or at full strength with soldiers who are only 50 percent effective. As individual and unit capabilities fall, battle fatigue may contribute not only to more battle fatigue casualties but also to higher rates of wounds and disease and nonbattle injures (DNBI).

e. The skill and courage of leaders at all levels are critical to success in operations across the full range of conflict. The chaos of combat places a premium on initiative, unit cohesion, and mental and physical preparedness of soldiers and units. While the importance of winning the first battle is great, the ability to fight sustained campaigns is vital to deterrence and to victory. In war, temporary battle fatigue casualties are inevitable but can be treated and returned to duty in or close to their units. In operations other than war (conflict), the enemy threat counts on psychological stress and misconduct stress behaviors to disable the defender. In operations other than war (conflict), drug and alcohol abuse, other violations of military discipline, and criminal acts must be prevented by strong leadership. Misconduct stress behaviors are dealt with through the legal system. Medical care and treatment are provided when necessary.

TABLE 1-1. Examples of Catastrophic Events During Peacetime and Operations Other Than War—Historic Incidents

- The crash at Gander, Newfoundland, of a contract airliner carrying home one-third of a battalion of the 101st Airborne Division from the Sinai Peacekeeping Mission.*
- The car-bombing by Shiite fanatics of the Marine Battalion's barracks at Beirut Airport, Lebanon,** and of the American Embassy in Beirut.
- The death by burning of many Fort Knox school children when a drunk driver crashed into their school bus.
- The hijacking of the ocean liner *Achille Lauro** and of several airliners* by Palestinian terrorists.
- The serious damaging of the destroyer USS *Stark* by an accidentally launched Iraqi missile in the Persian Gulf.*,**
- The shooting down of an Iranian civilian airliner in the Persian Gulf by the

cruiser *Vincennes*.***

- The crash of two Italian jets into the crowd of spectators at an air show in Ramstein, West Germany.****

- The explosion of a gun turret on the battleship *Iowa* during target practice,** and several fatal fires and crashes aboard submarines and aircraft carriers.**

- The crash of two California Army National Guard (CAARNG) helicopters while on drug interdiction service.#

- Disaster relief to South Florida following Hurricane Andrew**,## and operation Restore Hope in Somalia.###

---

   * 17th Medical Command, US Army, Europe, sent its Stress Management Team.
  ** The Navy SPRINT (Special Psychiatric Rapid Intervention Team) was deployed.
 *** The Board of Inquiry cited "combat stress" as primary cause of the error.
**** The mental health debriefing assisted survivors and care givers.
   # The CAARNG Medical Brigade sent a special Stress Control Team.
  ## The 10th Mountain, 24th Infantry, and 82nd Airborne Divisions' Mental Health Sections played important parts.
 ### The 10th Mountain Division's Mental Health Section and a new Combat Stress Control Detachment were deployed and debriefed Army and Marine units.

1-6. THE POTENTIAL HIGH-TECH BATTLEFIELD

United States Army planners have predicted what future high-tech combat could entail. This was demonstrated in the recent past with the world's confrontation with Iraq over the seizure of Kuwait. Based on the current world situation, such future battles are not unthinkable. The unprecedented debilitating effects of battlefield in the twenty-first century will demand even more attention to the preparation of soldiers, crews, and leaders for combat hardships. In such battlefields, the soldier will face many challenges.

    a. *Challenge of Isolation.* The first challenge is isolation. Units may experience periods of combat where forces are intermixed and lines of communications are broken. Units will experience feelings of uncertainty and helplessness from unpredictable strikes by long-range weapon systems. To make matters worse, these strikes may be inflicted by one's own forces in the confusion of battle. The certain use of smoke and obscurants will limit soldiers' vision, promoting feelings of separation, abandonment, and vulnerability.

b. *Challenge of Higher Rates of Casualties from Conventional, Nuclear, Biological, and Chemical Weapons/Agents.* The increased rate of destruction of potential future weaponry has both physical and psychological effects. Losing 40 to 60 percent of an entire unit in minutes or hours could leave the remaining soldiers incapacitated. The rapid and horrible death of their comrades and leaders could have a definite and detrimental effect on the mental stability of the unit. Surviving soldiers will have to be prepared to overcome the experience of mass human destruction. They will need to be trained to take over from those lost and to reshape units that can continue to fight.

c. *Challenge of Human-Technological Imbalance.* The emergence of new technologies has significantly increased the range of weapons, reduced reaction time, and changed conditions over which battles are fought. This new technology has the potential to exceed the capacity of human crews to fight.

• All-weather, day-and-night-capable vehicles which can operate for extended periods without resupply are limited only by the crews' need for sleep.

• High-probability-of-kill, direct-fire systems will be degraded over time by the stress and fatigue levels of the men aiming those weapons.

• Improved sensors and longer range weapons could exceed the capabilities of a tactical headquarters to plan and execute battles fought over expanded areas of operations.

• Short engagement times and the increased lethality of new weapons could overwhelm the ability of staffs to control and coordinate the overall battle.

Soldiers, leaders, and staffs will face problems of reduced efficiency and effectiveness when fighting over extended periods. These conditions will tend to neutralize the potential gains of new war-fighting technologies and force new approaches to the preparation and employment of soldiers, leaders, and staffs.

d. *Challenge of the Mental Rigors of Combat.* Armies must initiate training programs to help precondition soldiers to the mental rigors of combat. This is of vital importance as the potentially catastrophic effect of battle stress in future warfare becomes evident. The military force that does this best will have a decided edge in any war. Future combat will strain human endurance to unprecedented levels. If these challenges are left unchecked by poor mental and physical conditioning of soldiers, they could result in the disastrous failure of entire units. Failure to consider the human factors in an environment of increased lethality and uncertainty could cause a nation's concept of warfare to be irrelevant. With the miniaturization and spread of high-tech (and perhaps even of nuclear, biological, and chemical [NBC]) weapons, this can be just as true in operations other than war (conflict) as in war.

1-7. RESPONSIBILITIES FOR CONTROLLING COMBAT (CONFLICT) STRESS

a. *Unit Cohesiveness Development.* Rigorous, realistic training for war must go on continuously to assure unit readiness. Emphasis must be placed on establishing and maintaining cohesive units. Unit training and activities must emphasize development of soldier skills. This development should focus on building trust and establishing effective communication throughout the unit.

b. *Senior (Organizational) Leaders' Responsibilities.* The chain of command must ensure that the standards for military leadership are met. Senior leaders must provide the necessary information and resources to the junior leaders to control combat stress and to make stress work for the US Army and against the enemy. Senior leaders' responsibilities are listed in Table 1-2.

c. *Junior (Direct) Leaders' Responsibilities.* Junior leaders, and especially the NCOs, have the crucial business of applying the principles of stress control day-by-day, hour-by-hour, minute-by-minute. These responsibilities overlap with senior leaders' responsibilities but include parts that are fundamentally "sergeants' business," supported by the officers. See Table 1-3, page 16, for junior leaders' responsibilities.

d. *Staff Section Responsibilities.* Each element of the commander's staff (adjutant, intelligence, operations, logistics, and civil and public affairs [if present]) has its own area of responsibility that has particular relevance to stress control (see Table 1-4, pages 17–18). For example, the adjutant's responsibility for mail and decorations is more than just "nice to have." These are important stress control measures. Morale, welfare, and recreation opportunities, and even the use of Army bands, are valuable ways to sustain morale and combat readiness. For additional information on the role of Army bands, see Appendix C.

   e.   *Chaplains' Responsibilities.* Chaplains, especially those in unit ministry teams, have extremely important responsibilities. See Table 1-5 for chaplains' responsibilities. For additional information on the unit ministry teams, see Appendix D.

   f.   *Unit Medical Personnel's Responsibilities.* Unit medical personnel assist commanders and NCOs in the control of stressors. See Table 1-6, page 21, for combat stress control responsibilities.

TABLE 1-2. Senior Leaders' Responsibilities

- Be competent, committed, courageous, candid, and caring.
- Plan to accomplish the mission with as few losses as possible.
- Set the policy and command climate for stress control, especially to build teams with high unit cohesion.
- Serve as an ethical role model.
- Make "the bureaucracy" work for the troops.
- Assure resources to "take care of the troops."
- Plan for and conduct tough, realistic training to include live fires.
- Provide as much information as possible to the troops.
- Assure that medical and mental health/combat stress control personnel are assigned and trained with their supported units.
- Plan for combat stress control in all operations.
- Provide the junior leaders/NCOs with the necessary guidance.
- Ensure risk assessments are conducted prior to all training and combat operations.
- Supervise the junior leaders/NCOs and reward their success.
- Be visible.
- Lead all stress control measures by good example.
- Maintain (through positive leadership and, when necessary, with disciplinary action) the high standards of the international law of land warfare.

TABLE 1-3. Junior Leaders' Responsibilities—Combat Stress Control*

- Be competent, committed, courageous, candid, and caring.
- Build cohesive teams; integrate new personnel quickly.
- Cross-train soldiers wherever and whenever possible.
- Plan and conduct tough realistic training that replicates combat conditions, especially live fires.
- Take care of the troops (including the leaders).
- Assure physical fitness, nutrition, hydration, adequate clothing and shelter, and preventive medicine measures.
- Make and enforce sleep plans.
- Keep accurate information flowing down to the lowest level (and back up again); dispel rumors.
- Encourage sharing of resources and feelings.
- Conduct after-action debriefings routinely.
- Maintain (through positive leadership and, when necessary, with disciplinary action) the high standards of the international law of land warfare.
- Recommend exemplary soldiers for awards and decorations.
- Recognize excess stress early and give immediate support.
- Keep those stressed soldiers who can still perform their duties in the unit, and provide extra support and encourage them back to full effectiveness.
- Send those stressed soldiers who cannot get needed rest in their small unit back to a supporting element for brief sleep, food, hygiene, and limited duty, to return in 1 to 2 days.
- Refer temporarily unmanageable stress cases through channels for medical evaluation and treatment.
- Welcome recovered battle fatigue casualties back and give them meaningful work and responsibilities.

*Note that every soldier ultimately must be a junior (direct) leader. Each soldier must exercise self-leadership and control stress for self and others.

TABLE 1-4. Staff Responsibilities for Combat Stress Control

S1/G1 PERSONNEL

- Assure soldiers' pay, mail, and the availability of telephones when feasible.
- Assure personnel replacement, preferably with cohesive teams.
- Return recovered casualties to original units whenever possible.
- Assure rapid, accurate casualty reporting.
- Assist planning for medical care and evaluation.
- Assure bath, laundry, clothing replacement, comfort kits, and other like area/items with the S4.
- Plan morale/welfare/rest and recreation opportunities and facilities.
- Utilize army bands to sustain esprit, morale.
- Monitor in coordination with the S3/G3 cumulative stress in unit such as sleep loss, causalities, and number of new personnel replacements.
- Recommend rotation of units into reserve or formal reconstitution.
- Keep information flow open with rear detachments and family support groups.
- Collate statistics on misconduct behaviors (disciplinary and military police actions) which could be due to combat or other stress.
- Process timely awarding of individual and unit decorations and citations.
- Know locations and capabilities of combat stress control teams and coordinate with them as required.

S2/G2 INTELLIGENCE

- Disseminate information on enemy weapons' capabilities, tactics, and actions.
- Disseminate information on weather, terrain, and other potential stressors.
- Disseminate information on enemy troop concentration, capabilities, and likely courses of action.
- Ensure issue of appropriate clothing and equipment.
- Prevent unpleasant surprises.

S3/G3 OPERATIONS

- Encourage maximum dissemination of information about the tactical and operational plan, limited only by essential operational security.
- Consider stress issues and cumulative stress of units when making operational plans with S1.
- Plan rotation of units to allow sleep/respite.
- Schedule live fire and mission rehearsal training in the combat zone when feasible.
- Integrate combat stress control and psychological operations into the operational plan.

S4/G4 LOGISTICS

- Assure adequate food, water, ammunition, and fuel.
- Keep weapons systems and communication equipment functioning.
- Assure bath, laundry, clothing, and other like areas/items with S1/G1.
- Assure respectful handling of the dead.
- Assist with transport of battle fatigue casualties in general purpose vehicles.

S5/G5 CIVIL AFFAIRS

- Recognize and mediate stress issues between US personnel and the local population.
- Coordinate for host-nation support.

PUBLIC AFFAIRS

- Assure the unit gets proper recognition for its achievements in the US media.
- Assist the commander in determining information needs of soldiers.
- Assist the commander in message and product development.
- Facilitate communications channels.
- Serve as primary interface between the military and civilian media.

1-8. PRIMARY RESPONSIBILITY—COMBAT STRESS CONTROL/MENTAL HEALTH PERSONNEL

Combat stress control is the primary responsibility—in peace as well as in war—of the mental health team. While the chain of command and NCO chain of support have ultimate responsibility for stress control, the unit leaders must give primary attention to accomplishing their unit's mission. Headquarters staffs and unit chaplains and medical personnel also have other primary missions which must come first. Sustaining military performance, preventing stress casualties, and treating stress symptoms are the primary missions for Army combat stress control units and personnel.

a. *Combat Stress Control Organization.* As defined in Army Regulation (AR) 40-216, the mental health team consists of Army psychiatrists, clinical psychologists, social work officers, occupational therapy officers, psychiatric nurses, and their enlisted counterparts. Mental health personnel are organized into organic mental health sections in the main support medical companies of divisions and the medical companies of separate brigades. In both the corps and the COMMZ, the mental health sections are organic to the area support medical battalion. Mental health staff sections in the medical command, medical brigade, and medical group monitor and coordinate combat stress control support. The medical combat stress control units (companies and detachments) are a corps and COMMZ asset. They are designed to divide into mobile, modular combat stress control teams. The teams provide combat stress control support throughout the corps and routinely deploy forward to reinforce mental health section personnel in the division and brigade areas. The philosophy and the organizational and operational concept for combat stress control are reviewed in Appendix B.

b. *Combat Stress Control/Mental Health Team Responsibilities.* Table 1-7, page 22–23, summarizes the mission and responsibilities of combat stress control/mental health personnel in combat stress control.

1-9. EFFECTIVE COMBAT STRESS CONTROL PROGRAM

Without an effective combat stress control program, combat stress can be a "war-stopper" for our soldiers. This may be by way of a high number of battle fatigue casualties during and after intense critical battles. It may be by way of misconduct stress behaviors which undermine the objectives and the will to persist in operations other than war (conflict). Maximizing the amount of combat stress experienced by our forces is one of the main objectives of the enemy. An effective combat stress control program requires participation at all levels. It is implemented by command authority. It is supported by commanders, leaders, staffs, chaplains, physicians, and health care providers and should be facilitated by mental health/combat stress control personnel and units. Through these actions we can control the effects combat stress has on the accomplishment of unit missions by—

- Identifying and controlling stress factors (stressors).
- Reducing number of battle fatigue casualties and misconduct stress behaviors.
- Reducing recovery time for battle fatigue casualties.

An effective combat stress control program focuses the effects of combat stress toward increasing positive stress responses while decreasing disruptive stress. It reduces the possibilities of stress becoming a war-stopper for the US.

TABLE 1-5. Chaplains' Responsibilities for Combat Stress Control

- Provide religious support and the ministry of presence (being with the soldiers) to all soldiers in the unit.
- Advise command on spiritual, moral, and morale issues as a special staff officer.
- Help soldiers to be spiritually strong to face the moral and ethical dilemmas and paradoxes of human combat.
- Encourage soldiers to share feelings after combat.
- Encourage continued performance of duty.
- Recognize stress symptoms, provide immediate solace, and recommend further evaluation and treatment when appropriate.
- Know and provide information to unit leaders on combat stress control team locations and capabilities.
- Provide assistance with integrating recovered stress casualties back into their units.
- Minister to the sick and dying.
- Assist survivors with grief and bereavement.

TABLE 1-6. Unit Medical Personnel's Responsibilities for Combat Stress Control

- Advise and inform leaders and soldiers/patients on stress.
- Encourage healthy fitness of the soldiers, assist leaders with after-action debriefings, sleep plans, hygiene, nutrition, and hydration.
- Detect excess stress early and intervene when feasible, treat and release soldiers back to the small unit or to rest in the small unit's higher headquarters (1 to 2 days maximum) before returning to duty.
- Hold the stress cases who cannot return immediately to their units and give brief (1 to 3 day) restoration in medical holding facilities.
- Refer (evacuate) temporarily unmanageable stress cases but only to the next medical echelon or to the nearest combat stress control teams.
- Know and provide information to unit leaders on combat stress control team locations and capabilities.
- Provide transportation, if possible, for combat stress control personnel when they provide consultation to units.
- Be alert for stress symptoms in all physically injured and all soldiers (both return-to-duty and evacuated-to-CONUS cases) and initiate immediate treatment.
- Provide quality health service support in the form of preventive actions, routine care, emergency treatment, and convalescent care for return to duty or evacuation.

Note: When soldiers know that they will receive timely medical care if wounded, injured, or ill—that is a powerful stress controller.

TABLE 1-7. Combat Stress Control Unit and Mental Health/Combat Stress Control Personnel's Responsibilities

- Be the Army's organizational memory and advocate for stress control issues.
- Be proactive and mobile and present with the troops.
- Be identified with supported unit and trusted by its leaders.
- Provide consultation to leaders, chaplains, medical personnel, and staffs including—
  - Technical supervision and training.
  - Case evaluation and advice.
  - Personnel reliability screening.
  - Information briefings.
    - Identification of stressors.
    - Analysis of stressors.
    - Stress control techniques.
    - Sleep planning.
    - Suicide prevention.
    - Substance abuse prevention.
    - Family issues.
    - Other areas as required.
  - Staff planning for combat stress control in all operations, including peacetime.
  - Surveys of stress in the unit, its cohesion, and readiness.
  - Transition workshops; enhanced organizational function.
  - Coordination for unit, family support groups, and support agencies.
  - Emphasis on prevention of stress casualties and on treatment in or close to the unit.
  - Assisting the return to duty and reintegration of recovered casualties into their original or new units and jobs.
- Provide reorganization/reconstitution support for severely attrited units.
- Provide critical events debriefings following disasters or accidents.
- Provide proximate neuropsychiatric triage (sorting based on how far forward the overstressed soldier can be treated); separate other cases with serious physical or mental illness for evacuation.

- Supervise or provide 1- to 3-day restoration treatment for battle fatigue casualties at medical facilities close to the soldier's units.
- Provide longer reconditioning for slow-to-improve cases at a secure location, usually in the corps (for 4 to 14 days) and COMMZ (for up to 28 days) depending on the theater evacuation policy.
- Supervise or provide stabilization for acutely disruptive cases and evaluate for further treatment and either return to duty or evacuate to CONUS.

CHAPTER 2

STRESS AND COMBAT PERFORMANCE

SECTION I.
STRESS TERMINOLOGY AND THE
STRESS CONCEPT

2-1. INTRODUCTION.

The understanding of the stress process has been refined over time by research and experience, leaving some terms obsolete. This chapter establishes how the Army's combat stress control concept currently defines and interprets stress terminology.

2-2. UNDERSTANDING OF INTERACTIONS

   a.   *Stressors.* A stressor is any event or situation which requires a nonroutine change in adaptation or behavior. Often it is unfamiliar or creates conflict among motives within the individual. It may pose a challenge or a threat to the individual's well-being or self-esteem. Stressors may be positive or negative (for example, promotion to new responsibilities or threat of imminent death).

   b.   *Combat Stressors.* Combat stressors are any stressors occurring during the course of combat-related duties, whether due to enemy action or other sources. Combat duties do not necessarily involve being shot at and may be carried on even in "safe" areas far from the enemy. Many stressors in combat duties come from the soldier's own unit, leaders, and mission demands. They may also come from the conflict between mission demands and the soldier's home life.

   c.   *Stress.* Stress is the internal process of preparing to deal with a stressor. Stress involves the physiological reflexes which ready the body for fight or flight. Examples of those reflexes are increased nervous system arousal, release of adrenaline into the bloodstream, changes in blood flow to different parts of the body, and so forth. However, stress is not synonymous with arousal or anxiety. Stress involves physical and mental processes which, at times, suppress arousal and anxiety. Stress also involves the accompanying emotional responses and the automatic perceptual and cognitive processes for evaluating the uncertainty or threat. These automatic processes may be instinctive or learned.

d. *Stress Appraisal.* Stress may or may not involve conscious awareness of the threat, but the stressor must be perceived at some level to cause stress. The amount of stress experienced depends much on the individual's appraisal of the stressor and its context, even if that appraisal is wrong. The stress process includes psychological defenses which may filter the perception and appraisal to shield the individual from perceiving more threat than he is ready to tolerate.

e. *Physical Stressors Versus Mental Stressors.* A distinction can be made between those stressors which are physical and those which are mental.

(1) A physical stressor is one which has a direct effect on the body. This may be an external environmental condition or the internal physical/physiologic demands of the human body.

(2) A mental stressor is one in which only information reaches the brain with no direct physical impact on the body. This information may place demands on either the cognitive systems (thought processes) or the emotional system (feeling responses, such as anger or fear) in the brain. Often, reactions are evoked from both the cognitive and the emotional systems.

f. *Stress Behaviors.* These are stress-related actions that can be observed by others; for example, moving or keeping still, speaking or not speaking. The behaviors may be intended to overcome and turn off a stressor, to escape it, or to adapt to it. They may simply reflect or relieve the tension generated by the internal stress process. Any of these different types of stress behavior may be successful, unsuccessful, or not influence the stressful situation at all. They may make the stressor worse. They may resolve one stressor but create new stressors.

g.   *Combat Stress.* This is the complex and constantly changing result of all the stressors and stress processes inside the soldier as he performs the combat-related mission. At any given time in each soldier, stress is the result of the complex interaction of many mental and physical stressors.

2-3. DISCUSSION OF PHYSICAL VERSUS MENTAL STRESSORS

a.   Table 2-1 gives examples of the two types of physical stressors (environmental and physiological) and the two types of mental stressors (cognitive and emotional).

b.   The physical stressors evoke specific stress reflexes. For example, cold causes shivering and decreased blood flow to skin and extremities; heat causes sweating and increased blood flow to skin. These stress reflexes can maintain internal balance and comfort up to a point but then may be exceeded.

c.   The distinction, however, between physical and mental stressors is rarely clear cut.

(1) Mental stressors can also produce the same stress reflexes as do some physical stressors; for example, decreased blood flow to skin, increased sweating, adrenaline release, and pupil size. These reflexes can markedly increase or decrease the individual's vulnerability to specific physical stressors. The mental stressors also presumably cause changes in brain chemistry (involving the neurotransmitter chemicals in the brain).

(2) Physical stressors are also mental stressors when they provide information to the brain which creates a mental demand or poses a threat to well-being. Even if a physical stressor is not a threat to life and health, the discomfort, distraction, and performance degradation it causes may be emotionally upsetting. Therefore, physical stressors, too, can produce the nonspecific arousal reflexes. Heat, cold, dehydration, toxic chemicals, and other physical stressors can also interfere directly with brain functioning; they can impair perceptual and cognitive mental abilities, thus increasing the stresses. Light, noise, discomfort, and anxiety-provoking information may interfere with sleep, which is essential to maintain brain efficiency and mental performance over time.

d. Because of this intermeshing of physical and mental stressors and stress reflexes, no great effort needs to be invested in distinguishing them in military contexts until the physical stressors and stress reflexes become so severe that they warrant specific (and perhaps

TABLE 2-1. Types of Physical and Mental Stressors

PHYSICAL STRESSORS	MENTAL STRESSORS
ENVIRONMENTAL	COGNITIVE
Heat, cold, or wetness	Information: too much or too little
Vibration, noise, blast	Sensory overload versus deprivation
Hypoxia (insufficient oxygen), fumes, poisons, chemicals	Ambiguity, uncertainty, isolation
Directed-energy weapons/devices	Time pressure versus waiting
Ionizing radiation	Unpredictability
Infectious agents/disease	Rules of engagement, difficult judgments
Skin irritants or corrosives	Organizational dynamics
Physical work	Hard choices versus no choices
Bright light, darkness, haze, and obscuration	Recognition of impaired functioning
Difficult or arduous terrain	
PHYSIOLOGICAL	EMOTIONAL
Sleep debt	Fear- and anxiety-producing threats (of injury, disease, pain, failure, loss, personal or mission failure)
Dehydration	
Malnutrition, poor hygiene	Grief-producing losses (bereavement)
Muscular and aerobic fatigue	Resentment, anger- and rage-producing frustration, threat, loss, and guilt
Impaired immune system	
Overuse or underuse of muscles, organ systems	Boredom-producing inactivity
Illness or injury	Conflicting motives (worries about home, divided loyalties)
	Spiritual confrontation or temptation causing loss of faith
	Interpersonal feelings

Note: The above stressors may act singly or interact with each other to be combat stressors.

emergency) protective measures and treatment. Prior to that stage, unit leaders and medical and mental health personnel should assume that both physical and mental stresses are usually present and interacting within all unit personnel. Guidelines for controlling both physical and mental stressors at the same time should be contained in the tactical standing operating procedure (TSOP), if possible.

2-4. POSITIVE STRESS

a.   Stress is not necessarily bad or harmful. Positive stress (or eustress) is that degree of stress which is necessary to sustain and improve tolerance to stress without overdoing the stress experience. Some level of stress is helpful and even necessary to health. This is especially clear for some physical stressors to which the body can acclimatize. To achieve greater tolerance or acclimatization to a physical stressor, a progressively greater exposure is required. The exposure should be sufficient to produce more than the routine stress reflexes. Well-known examples of acclimatization are heat acclimatization, cardiovascular (aerobic) fitness, and muscle strength. These examples are so important to combat stress control that they are worth reviewing. The process of improving tolerance to stressors through progressive exposure to those stressors will also be true of cognitive-emotional stressors.

(1) *Heat acclimatization.* You cannot become fully acclimatized to heat by just lying around in hot conditions. You have to perform physical exercise in the heat to stress the body's temperature regulation system. At first, the body may overreact with excessive sweating and heart rate. As acclimatization occurs, the body becomes more efficient at cooling itself. However, acclimation has a maximum level. If you stop exercising in the heat, you will gradually lose the acclimatization you have gained. Mission-oriented protective posture (MOPP) training should be considered as a part of the acclimatization program.

(2) *Aerobic fitness.* It is well known that you can become aerobically fit only by exerting yourself to progressively greater degrees of physical effort. One way is to enter into 20-minute (or more) exercise programs of jogging, running, bicycling, swimming, or special aerobic exercises each day. Any physical effort which sufficiently

raises heart rate and respiratory rate and works up a sweat for 20 minutes or more will increase your tolerance. In other words, you must stress the system. After doing that for several days, the same effort raises heart rate and sweating only a little. You become less short of breath, and the effort seems much easier. To become more aerobically fit, you have to increase the work stressor even more until the body again shows the stress of increased heart rate, shortness of breath, and sweating. If you stop exercising aerobically for weeks or months, your improved aerobic fitness will gradually be lost.

(3) *Muscle strength.* Body builders increase their muscle mass by lifting progressively heavier weights or working against progressively greater resistance on exercise machines. In order to increase muscle strength, you have to increase the stressor (the weight lifted) and the stress (the physiological increased effort within the muscle cells). After the muscle has become accustomed to lifting a given weight, it no longer seems like a great effort. There is little stress taking place in the muscle. The muscle will merely maintain its strength and not get any stronger with repeated exposure. If you stop doing even that amount of lifting, your muscles will get flabby again over time. A good maxim is, "If you do not use it, you will lose it."

b.   It is important to understand that stressors which overstrain the adaptive capability of the body (whether or not they cause pain) do not hasten acclimatization or increase tolerance to the stressor. They often retard it and may even permanently impair future acclimatization. Consider the examples of the physical stressors discussed above.

(1) Heat acclimatization is not speeded by getting heat cramps or heat exhaustion. Neither is it significantly slowed, although the person's self-confidence and motivation to try again may be impaired. However, people who are driven to the stage of heatstroke and survive will forever be physically less tolerant to heat. They will be more likely to develop heatstroke in the future if exposed to heat.

(2) Runners or body builders who push too hard early in training may not feel severe pain at the time. Hours later, however, they may develop muscle swelling, ache, and stiffness. At best, this will take days to recover to the point where the athlete can even continue with

the exercise regimen. At worst, the damaged muscles may break down and release the substance myoglobin into the bloodstream which can permanently damage or destroy the kidneys. Excessive painful stress on bones, joints, and ligaments does not make them grow stronger but instead causes stress fractures, sprains, tears, and other damage that may require months of reduced activity to heal.

(3) The issue for the master fitness trainers is how to keep the physical work stressors and stress in the positive or eustress range which increases strength and fitness. They must control the stressors and stress so they are not extreme—too little or too much.

★   ★   ★

WARNING
Unconditioned, unacclimatized troops should not be overextended in training as this could cause severe injury or even death. A special physical training program will be required.

★   ★   ★

c.   Positive stress also applies to mental stressors (cognitive and emotional), as well as to physical stressors (environmental and physiological). Appropriate exposure to mental/emotional stressors is necessary to increase tolerance to them.

(1) Armies have known for centuries about the positive effects of stress in preparing soldiers for combat. In old-style basic training (prior to 1970), the drill sergeant deliberately made himself more fearsome than death itself so that the trainee would learn to respond automatically, even in a state of terror. That technique is not useful today because modern war requires more small unit cohesion, trust between leaders and those led, and initiative even on the part of the junior enlisted soldier. The modern drill sergeant must, instead, require the trainees to meet difficult (stressful) standards and work with the trainees to assure that they master them. The result is a well-earned sense of confidence in self, comrades, and leaders that can be applied to future demands.

(2) The Army knows that airborne and air assault training are not just intended to teach the skills needed to arrive on a battlefield after jumping from a low-flying aircraft or repelling from a helicopter. Their greater value comes from requiring soldiers to confront and master their extremely strong, instinctive fear of heights under circumstances which are deliberately stressful at the time. During training, the fear builds self-confidence and a sense of special identity on completion. (In fact, the training itself is not exceedingly dangerous, statistically speaking. However, the possibility of death does exist if you are extremely unlucky or fail to do the task correctly. This can contribute to additional stress.)

(3) Ranger school is a clear example of the Army's recognition of the benefits of positive stress. A generic ranger course objective would read: Perform complex and difficult physical and mental task under great pressure, sleep loss, water and food deprivation, and physical fatigue. No one coasts through ranger school. If anyone seems to be coasting through, the trained ranger cadre will increase the demand on that person until he, too, reaches the stage of stress where he realizes he cannot get through it all alone. Ranger school teaches small teams and their rotating leaders how to control stress in all the team members so the team accomplishes the mission. The training gives the individual soldier confidence, but even more, an awareness of how stress works in oneself and others. It teaches stress control, not stress reduction. Often the need for the team and its individual members is to play different mental and physical stressors against each other. This is done by increasing some stressors while decreasing others to keep the team on its mission and to keep individual soldiers from giving up.

d.   To some degree, acclimatization to mental (cognitive/emotional) stressors also shares that "use it or lose it" feature which is true for adaptation to physical stressors. The airborne-qualified trooper may experience more unpleasant stress symptoms when jumping after not having jumped for many months. The physician may find the stress unexpectedly higher when performing a potentially risky patient-care procedure that was once so frequently practiced that it had seemed to involve no stress at all but which has not been performed for some time. However, the memory of successfully mastering the stressor in the past usually speeds up the return of adaptation.

e.   Tolerance to mental stressors is increased by successfully facing and mastering similar stressors (just as tolerance to physical stressors is). However, being overwhelmed by emotional or mental stress may temporarily or permanently impair future tolerance (just as exceeding the ability to cope with physical stressors may). Up to a point, mental stress (even uncomfortable mental stress) may increase tolerance to future stress without any current impairment. A higher level may cause temporary overstrain but may heal as strong or stronger than ever with rest and restorative processing. More severe overstrain, however, may permanently weaken tolerance to future mental stress. As with some cases of damage from physical stress, the harm done by mental stress may not be apparent at the time. It may only be apparent later. There is reason to believe that immediate preventive measures or treatment can greatly reduce the potential for chronic disability, even in cases of extreme emotional overstrain.

2-5. RELATIONSHIP OF STRESS TO TASK PERFORMANCE

Stress is an internal process which presumably evolves because it helps the individual to function better, stay alive, and cope successfully with stressors. However, there is an optimal range of arousal (or motivation or stress) for any given task.

a.   If there is too little arousal, the job is done haphazardly or not at all because the individual is easily distracted, makes errors of omission, or falls asleep. If arousal becomes too intense, the individual may be too distractible or too focused on one aspect of the task. He may have difficulty with fine motor coordination and with discriminating when and how to act. If the individual is unfamiliar with his own stress reflexes and perceives them as dangerous (or incapacitating, or as a threat to self-esteem), the stress itself can become a stressor and magnify itself.

b.   With extreme arousal, the individual may freeze (become immobile or petrified by fear). Alternately, he may become agitated and flee in disoriented panic. If stress persists too long, it can cause physical and mental illnesses. Extreme stress with hopelessness can even

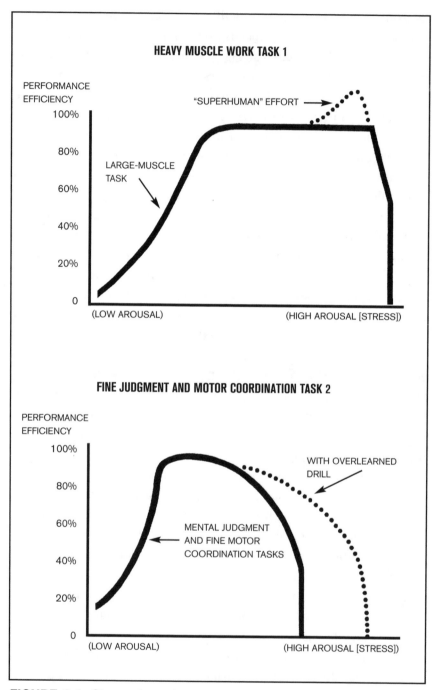

FIGURE 2-1. Change in performance with increasing arousal (stress) for two types of tasks.

result in rapid death, either due to sympathetic nervous system over-stimulation (such as stroke or heart attack) or due to sympathetic nervous system shutdown (not simply exhaustion). An individual giving up can literally stop the heart from beating.

c.   The original purpose of the stress reaction was to keep the person alive. The military requirement for the stress process is different. It is to keep the soldier in that range of physiological, emotional, and cognitive mobilization which best enables him to accomplish the military mission, whether that contributes to individual survival or not. This optimal range of stress differs from task to task. Tasks which require heavy but gross muscular exertion are performed best at high levels of arousal (Figure 2-1). Tasks that require fine muscle coordination and clear thinking (such as walking point on a booby-trapped jungle trail, or distinguishing subtle differences between friendly and enemy targets in a night-vision gun sight) or that require inhibiting action (such as waiting alertly in ambush) will be disrupted unless the stress process is kept finely tuned. If the stress process allows too much or too little arousal or if arousal does not lessen when it is no longer needed, stress has become harmful.

2-6. FATIGUE

Fatigue means weariness and/or decreased performance capability due to hard or prolonged work or effort. It reflects the stage where the energy mobilized by the stress process is beginning to run down. If the effort continues, the fatigue can build to the point of exhaustion.

a.   Fatigue can be produced by both physical and mental tasks. A well-known example of physical fatigue is muscle tiredness. This can be limited to specific muscles which have been overworked. Another example is aerobic fatigue (where the whole body is short of oxygen and perhaps blood sugar, is probably overheated, and is wanting to rest).

b.   Sleep loss produces a different kind of fatigue which is primarily mental. The sleep-deprived person has trouble keeping his mind focused although he has no decrease in muscular or aerobic work capacity. People with sleep-loss fatigue usually appear tired and slowed down, or they may also be speeded up, hyperactive, and irritable.

c.   Continued mental effort on a specific task, whether it is a task requiring much thinking or constant attention, produces mental fatigue. That is, performance gets progressively worse with time, and the person wishes he could stop to do something else. Even a few minutes of break, while the mind does some quite different mental tasks, substantially relieves the mental fatigue and improves the performance.

d.   Physical illness can also bring on fatigue. People who have ever had the flu or even just a cold know how quickly one tires. They only want to rest or sleep.

e.   Intense emotions also produce fatigue. This is especially true of anxiety and fear because they arouse the fight or flight reflexes of the physical stress process. This will be discussed later in justifying the use of the term *battle fatigue*.

f.   The level of fatigue experienced may be influenced by—
• Work intensity.
• Task difficulty.
• Duration of sustained effort.
• General well-being of the individual.

Fatigue can also be influenced by the level of preparedness to perform the specific task.

(1) For physical fatigue: A marathon runner may have strong legs, superb aerobic fitness, great health, and self-confidence, but too little arm and shoulder strength to be able to chin himself even once before being stopped by fatigue.

(2) For emotional fatigue: A healthy, confident soldier may have learned to carry his Dragon missile and guide it to its target easily in peacetime training. But if he has never learned to control his own fear, he may find himself too quickly fatigued to even carry the weight, let alone keep the missile on target for 10 seconds while under real, lethal enemy fire. He may, however, still be able to perform simple tasks. In WWII, the following observations and conclusion were made:

(a) In the fighting for Kwajalein Atoll, troops were halted three times by enemy fire. Their energy was exhausted even though they suffered no casualties and had moved fewer than two miles. In the Normandy invasion, a strong infantry company with many vigorous young men hit the beach still fresh. Under intense fire, they found they had to drag their heavy machine guns across the beach a few feet at a time; when in training, they had been able to carry the same loads on the run.

(b) The Army reached the following conclusion from those observations: Fear and fatigue affect the body in similar ways. Fear, like physical work, drains the body of energy. This creates a self-perpetuating cycle. The overloaded soldier, feeling tired, becomes more susceptible to fear. The more fearful he becomes, the weaker he feels, and the more quickly he becomes fatigued.

2-7. STAGES OF ADAPTATION TO A THREATENING SITUATION

a.   The stage of alarm (usually brief) is when the fight or flight response is extremely active. Performance is likely to be impaired unless the soldiers' responses are simple and instinctive (like running or freezing) or well drilled.

b.   The stage of resistance is achieved if the subject successfully copes with the threat. The overarousal moderates and the sufferer begins to actively try to overcome or escape the stressor or to adapt to it. Performance is often enhanced in the stage of resistance. If the stressor is mastered or adapted to, the person either returns to the baseline level of stress or may have some residual stress while working through the unpleasant memories and their long-term implications.

c.   The stage of exhaustion may occur if the victim of stress is unable to escape, overcome, or tolerate a severe stressor. Performance deteriorates and may cease altogether. The victim may develop a stress-related illness and can even die of stress.

SECTION II.
COMBAT PERFORMANCE AND
COMBAT STRESS BEHAVIORS

2-8. PHASES OF ADAPTATION TO COMBAT

During the first time in battle for soldiers, their combat performance is usually lower than it was in precombat training. The novice soldiers are also at relatively high risk of being killed or wounded. This is partly because they have not yet learned to identify and respond automatically to the true dangers (such as the specific sounds of incoming artillery or mortar rounds). Under extreme stress, they may experience difficulty with focusing their attention and remembering what they were taught in training. Their ineffectiveness may also be caused by fear-induced fatigue. First-battle soldiers are at high risk of becoming battle fatigue casualties. Soldiers in their first time under fire are likely to experience high anxiety (the stages of alarm) (see Figure 2-2[A]). Poor showing on first exposure to real battle can be reduced by providing tough, realistic training (especially battle drills under high stress), but it cannot be totally prevented.

a.   *The Experienced Veteran.* If the soldier does not become a casualty in the first battle, his combat skills will improve quickly over the next few days. His skills continue to improve gradually over the next weeks until he is as good as he can get. An experienced soldier gains confidence in his skill, comrades, and leaders (see Figure 2-2[B]). For him, the stage of alarm is mostly in anticipation. He responds selectively and automatically to the truly dangerous sounds and cues of the battlefield. When the action starts, he immediately achieves the stage of resistance and is remarkably calm as he focuses on his job. However, the veteran is likely to have a considerable rebound of arousal and anxiety when the fight is over. Not all veteran soldiers ever achieve the state of really low fear in action. Some drop to mid levels, yet still perform their duties effectively.

b.   *Sustainment of Optimal Combat Skills.* Combat skills and high stress tolerance are maintained when frequent successful combat actions occur. If losses in the unit remain low, the veteran can maintain his optimal combat skills for many months. If there is a prolonged cease-fire or if the skilled soldier leaves the combat zone on individual R&R, there may be a brief drop in performance on his return to battle. That drop would be accompanied by a return of the anxiety pattern shown by new soldiers (Figure 2-2[A]) but the anxiety is much briefer. This would be like the anxiety felt by the airborne-qualified soldier who is making a jump after not having done so for many months. Predictably, the experienced veteran will regain his combat edge quickly upon returning to battle.

c. *The Overstressed Veteran.* If the unit suffers many casualties, however, and the chance of surviving a long war seems poor, the experienced soldier's combat performance begins to decline. It can occur after 14 to 21 days of cumulative combat or even after only a few days of extremely heavy losses. The overstressed veteran becomes more careful, loses initiative, and may be indecisive when he needs to act quickly. Figure 2-2(C) shows the anxiety pattern of an overstressed soldier who is doubting his chances of survival. There were too many close calls in the last battle; too many of his friends were killed (slowly over time or quickly). Under such stress, he feels his own skills are slipping, and it is just a matter of time before he, too, will surely be killed or maimed. Unless he is given the opportunity and help to reduce arousal level and regain some hope, he will soon fail.

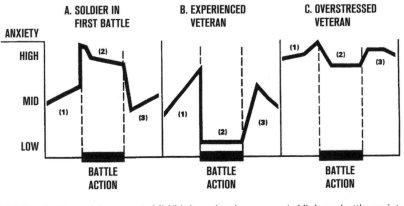

1. Mid prebattle anxiety: worried about unknown.
2. High fear in battle: trouble doing job, feels incompetent.
3. Rapid relief over surviving.

1. Mid/high prebattle anxiety: knows the risk.
2. Low fear in action: concentrates on job skills.
3. Rebound anxiety: looks back, sees close calls.

1. High prebattle anxiety: dreads the risk.
2. High fear in action: unable to control stress, awareness of risk.
3. High rebound: preoccupied with close calls and guilt that others were killed.

FIGURE 2-2. Anxiety, fear, and arousal at different stages in combat tour.

d. *Decline of Combat Skills.* How quickly performance declines will usually be related to how many casualties have occurred and how close the soldier was to them (both physically and emotionally). The decline may be hastened or slowed by leadership, unit, scenario, and home front factors such as those discussed in later chapters and in Appendix A.

e. *Restoration of Combat Skills.* Rest and recuperation, preferably with other soldiers in the unit, can substantially restore combat proficiency. Rest would also substantially return the anxiety pattern to that of the experienced veteran (Figure 2-2[B]). The recuperation can be accomplished with the help of the medical and combat stress control/mental health personnel at a medical restoration or reconditioning facility.

2-9. COMBAT STRESS BEHAVIORS

a. *Combat Stress Behaviors.* Combat stress behavior is the generic term which covers the full range of behaviors in combat, from behaviors that are highly positive to those that are totally negative. Table 2-2 provide a listing of positive stress responses and behaviors, plus two types of dysfunctional combat stress behaviors—those which are labeled misconduct stress behaviors and those which are labeled battle fatigue.

b. *Positive Combat Stress Behaviors.* Positive combat stress behaviors include the heightened alertness, strength, endurance, and tolerance to discomfort which the fight or flight stress response and the stage of resistance can produce when properly in tune. Examples of positive combat stress behaviors include the strong personal bonding between combat soldiers and the pride and self-identification which they develop with the combat unit's history and mission (unit esprit). These together form unit cohesion—the binding force that keeps soldiers together and performing the mission in spite of danger and death. The ultimate positive combat stress behaviors are acts of extreme courage and action involving almost unbelievable strength. They may even involve deliberate self-sacrifice. Positive combat stress behaviors can be brought forth by sound military training (drill), wise personnel polices, and good leadership. The results are behaviors which are rewarded with praise and perhaps with medals for individual valor and/or unit citations. The positive combat stress behaviors are discussed further in Chapter 3.

c. *Misconduct Stress Behaviors.* Examples of misconduct stress behaviors are listed in the center column of Table 2-2. These range from minor breaches of unit orders or regulations to serious violations of the Uniform Code of Military Justice (UCMJ) and perhaps the Law of Land Warfare. As misconduct stress behaviors, they are most likely to occur in poorly trained, undisciplined soldiers. However, they can also be committed by good, even heroic, soldiers under extreme combat stress. Misconduct stress behavior can be prevented by stress control measures, but once serious misconduct has occurred, it must be punished to prevent further erosion of discipline. Combat stress, even with heroic combat performance, cannot justify criminal misconduct. See Chapter 4 for a discussion of misconduct stress behaviors.

d. *Battle Fatigue.* Battle fatigue is also called combat stress reaction or combat fatigue. See Table 2-2 for examples of battle fatigue. Those battle fatigue behaviors which are listed near the top may accompany excellent combat performance and are often found in heroes, too. These are normal, common signs of battle fatigue. Those that follow are listed in descending order to indicate progressively more serious or warning signs. Warning signs deserve immediate attention by the leader, medic, or buddy to prevent potential harm to the soldier, others, or the mission. Warning signs do not necessarily mean the soldier must be relieved of duty or evacuated if they respond quickly to helping actions. However, soldiers may need evaluation at medical treatment facilities to rule out other physical or mental illness. If the symptoms of battle fatigue persist and make the soldier unable to perform duties reliably, then medical treatment facilities, such as clearing stations and specialized combat stress control teams, can provide restorative treatment. At this point, the soldier is a battle fatigue casualty. For those cases, prompt treatment close to the soldier's unit provides the best potential for returning the soldier to duty. See Chapter 5 for a detailed discussion of battle fatigue.

TABLE 2-2. Combat Stress Behaviors

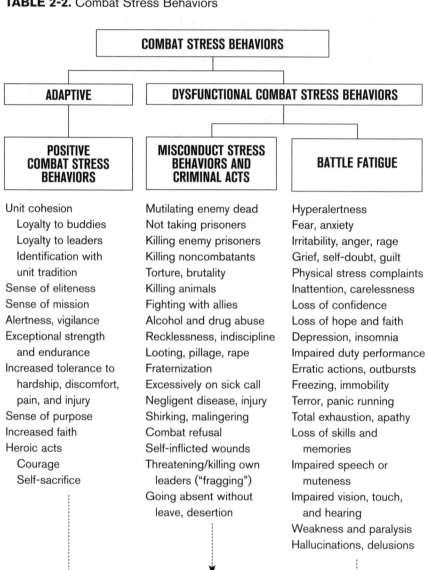

2-10. OVERLAPPING OF COMBAT STRESS BEHAVIORS

The distinction between positive combat stress behaviors, misconduct stress behaviors, and battle fatigue is not always clear. Indeed, the three categories of combat stress behaviors may overlap, as diagrammed in Figure 2-3. Soldiers with battle fatigue may show misconduct stress behaviors and vice versa. Heroes who exemplify the positive combat stress behaviors may suffer symptoms of battle fatigue and may even be battle fatigue casualties before or after their heroic deeds. Excellent combat soldiers may commit misconduct stress behaviors in reaction to the stressors of combat before, during, or after their otherwise exemplary performance. Combat stress, even with good combat behavior, does not excuse criminal acts. However, it could be taken into account as an extenuating circumstance for minor (noncriminal) infractions or in determining nonjudicial punishment under Article 15, UCMJ, for minor offenses.

2-11. POST-TRAUMATIC STRESS DISORDER

Post-traumatic stress symptoms are normal responses after extremely abnormal and distressing events.

    a.   *Post-Traumatic Stress Disorder Signs and Symptoms.* As with

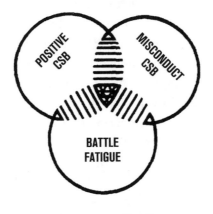

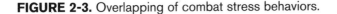

FIGURE 2-3. Overlapping of combat stress behaviors.

battle fatigue, post-traumatic stress symptoms come in normal/common and warning signs. These signs and symptoms do not necessarily make the sufferer a casualty or deserve the label of disorder. It is normal for the survivor of one or more horrible events to have painful memories; to have anxiety (perhaps with jumpiness or being on guard); to feel guilt (over surviving or for real acts of omission or commission); and to dream unpleasant dreams about it. This becomes PTSD only when either the pain of the memories or the actions the person takes to escape the memories (such as substance abuse, avoidance of reminders, social estrangement, and withdrawal) interfere with occupational or personal life goals.

b. *Post-Traumatic Stress Disorder Preventive Measures.* As with battle fatigue, there is no virtue in suffering, ignoring, neglecting, or hiding post-traumatic stress symptoms. The normal/common signs deserve routine preventive measures, such as talking out and working through the painful memories. The warning signs certainly deserve this attention, as self-aid, buddy aid, and leader aid. Good preventive measures can head off true PTSD which might not show up until years after the incident.

c. *Relationship Between Post-Traumatic Stress Disorder and Battle Fatigue.* While PTSD and battle fatigue obviously share much in common, by definition, symptoms are not PTSD until the trauma is over (post). Therefore, this diagnosis should not be made while the soldier continues in, or is expected to return quickly to, the combat mission. As the dotted lines (Table 2-2) show, PTSD can follow battle fatigue (especially if inadequately or incorrectly treated). Israeli studies confirm earlier observations that immediate, far-forward treatment and return to duty protect battle fatigue casualties against subsequent PTSD. Premature evacuation of battle fatigue casualties often results in chronic PTSD. However, most cases of acute, chronic, and delayed PTSD after a war were not battle fatigue casualties during the battles.

d. *Relationship Between Post-Traumatic Stress Disorder and Misconduct Stress Behavior.* Post-traumatic stress disorder often follows misconduct stress behaviors. It may occur in—

• The victims of others' misconduct.

- Those who committed misconduct under stress and are haunted by guilt later.
- Those who were passive or reluctant participants.
- Those who simply observed severe misconduct and its human consequences.
- Those who were involved as rescuers or care givers.

e. *Post-Traumatic Stress Disorder and Positive Combat Stress Behavior.* Post-traumatic stress disorder can also occur in soldiers (or veterans and civilians) who showed no maladaptive stress behaviors at the time of the trauma and who showed positive, even heroic, combat stress behaviors. Even heroes can feel delayed grief and survivor guilt for lost buddies or be haunted by the memory of the enemy soldiers they killed in battle.

f. *Leader Responsibilities to Prevent Post-Traumatic Stress Disorder.* During the conflict, commanders and NCOs have the additional responsibility of preventing or minimizing subsequent PTSD. The

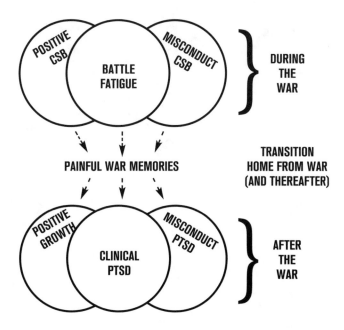

FIGURE 2-4. Relation between combat stress behaviors and PTSD.

most important preventive measure is routine after-action debriefing by small teams after any difficult operation (see Chapter 6 for additional discussion). Critical event debriefings led by trained debriefing teams should be scheduled following exceptionally traumatic events. Recommended leader actions are provided in Appendix A. When units or individual soldiers redeploy home from combat, leaders should debrief them and help prepare them for the transition. As Figure 2-4 illustrates, painful memories do not have to become clinical PTSD or misconduct stress behaviors. They can be accepted and diverted into positive growth. Chapter 6 gives more information on PTSD and its prevention and treatment.

CHAPTER 3

POSITIVE COMBAT STRESS BEHAVIORS

3-1. INTRODUCTION

Combat and war bring out the best and the worst in human beings. The direction which a combat stress behavior takes, positive or negative, results from the interaction of the physiological and social context in which the stress occurs and the physiologic stress response (preparing the body for fight or flight). The purpose of good military leadership, discipline, and training is to bring out the best while preventing the worst.

3-2. INCREASED ALERTNESS, STRENGTH, ENDURANCE—EXHILARATION

a   The physiological arousal caused by the stress process feels very good when it is optimal. Soldiers describe it with words such as thrill, exhilaration, adrenaline rush, and high. The resulting sense of focused alertness, heightened strength and endurance, and the feeling of competence (ready for instant response) is called being on a hair-trigger or on the razor's edge. It gives its possessors the winning edge.

b.   Combat veterans may remember war and their missions in it as the most exciting, most meaningful time in their lives—the high peak against which later life may seem flat and dull. Veterans returning from combat may have an experience not unlike withdrawal from addiction to stimulant drugs—a period of apathy and boredom, perhaps even of depression, during which they may be inclined to deliberately indulge in dangerous activity for the thrill of it.

3-3. GAMESMANSHIP AND SPORTSMANSHIP

a. Combat has been described as the Great Game. (Conversely, organized sports have been called the moral substitute for war.) Many tribal or clan-based cultures have practiced raids, ambushes, and skirmishes against other tribes for the thrill of the lethal game, valuing the loot more as trophies and proof of valor than for its material worth. Many fought carefully to avoid total victory because then they would have no worthy enemies left to fight.

b. From the sense of war as an honorable sport and of the enemy as an honorable opponent arose self-imposed rules of fair play or chivalry. These rules have slowly become the Law of Land Warfare.

c. With organized civilization, wars intensified and were more often fought for victory and total dominance. The sense of battle as an exciting game continues at many levels, even in modern conflict. For many soldiers, not only stopping enemy machines but also killing individually-targeted enemies still gives the thrill of the successful hunt.

d. With conscript armies and the increasing mechanization and depersonalization of combat, the game metaphor may be rejected by the frontline soldiers. This rejection occurs usually only after they have suffered bitter experiences from having tried to play the game. The battle-hardened and weary veterans may still view combat as the great game among themselves. These veterans resent having others who do not share the risk see them as only players, or treat the deaths of their buddies as nothing more than a normal part of the game.

3-4. SENSE OF ELITENESS AND DESIRE FOR RECOGNITION

a. *Sense of Eliteness.* Combat veterans who have achieved a high level of combat-stimulated proficiency and self-confidence are likely to consider themselves and their unit elite. They walk with pride and may expect special consideration or deference from others less elite. They are likely to want to do things their way rather than by the book. They may adopt special emblems, insignias, or TSOPs which set them apart. Up to some degree, this eliteness is a positive combat stress behavior which enhances combat performance. However, it is also likely to irritate others, both peers and superiors in the chain of command.

The latter recognize and adhere to the importance of uniformity and fairness (not showing favoritism) as key factors in sustaining military discipline and common purpose. The higher chain of command must mediate between these two legitimate positions (eliteness and uniformity) to gain the benefits of each. This is done with as few as possible of each position's negative side effects.

b. *Desire for Recognition.* Most soldiers desire public and long-lasting recognition for their hard work, suffering, and bravery. Awards and decorations are primarily given for this reason. Because the desire for recognition is so strong, it is important that the chain of command be perceived as awarding recognition properly and fairly. Failure to award recognition fairly (or failure to be perceived as awarding recognition fairly) can have long-term consequences on morale and stress within a unit. Most soldiers accept the fact that not all acts of heroism will be noticed. They acknowledge that receiving an award/decoration depends not only on the heroic act but on who observed it. It also depends on the leader to write the documentation. Commanders will differ in their policy regarding the criteria for the different award. It is desirable to give everyone positive motivation by making awards and decorations accessible, but if they are too easy to get, they quickly lose their value. This devaluation creates resentment in those who most deserve the special recognition. For this reason, higher command may set numerical limits on how many of each type of decoration that each subordinate commander may award. Good leaders will try to assure that exceptional performance and heroic acts get recognized based on merit. It is important that awards be distributed across the ranks, commensurate with performance without regards for race or gender. When it is not possible to give everyone a medal, leaders may write letters of commendation or, as a minimum, give a strong verbal "well done" for exceptional performance.

3-5. SENSE OF PURPOSE

War, with its stakes of life or death, victory or defeat, tends to create a sense of patriotism and common purpose that overcomes petty complaints, jealousies, and self-interest. This is true not only in combat soldiers but also in rear area troops. It is even true among the civilians on the home front, provided they are emotionally mobilized and behind the war effort. They, too, may look back on that time of common purpose and unity with nostalgia.

3-6. INCREASED RELIGIOUS FAITH

It is probably an exaggeration to say that there are "no atheists in the foxhole," but many soldiers and civilians do find that danger, and especially the unpredictable danger of modern war, stimulates a new or stronger need for faith in God. If this is fused with a sense of purpose in fulfilling God's will, it may lead to living a better life, increased dedication to duty, and attempting to make the world better in spite of the horrors and evils seen in war. In some cultures and religions, acceptance of God's will, fatalism, faith in the afterlife, or the reward for dying in a holy cause may also contribute to exceptional bravery and disregard for death. However, such faith dos not always promote good tactical common sense. It can lead to unproductive loss of life unless guided by sound leadership.

3-7. PERSONAL BONDING

While patriotism and sense of purpose will get American soldiers to the battlefield, the soldiers' own accounts (and many systematic studies) testify that what keeps them there amid the fear of death and mutilation is, above all else, their loyalty to their fellow soldiers. This loyalty was first called *cohesion* by Ardant Du Picq (the 19th century French officer and student of men in battle).

a.   Cohesion literally means stick together. The objective measure of cohesion is whether a soldier will choose to stay with his buddies and face discomfort and danger when given the opportunity or temptation to choose comfort and safety. The extreme measure of cohesion is willingness to die with fellow soldiers rather than leave them to die alone, or to choose certain death (as by throwing oneself on a hand grenade) in order to save their lives.

b.   Bonding within the combat team is itself a positive combat stress behavior. Working together under stress to overcome difficulty and discomfort in order to accomplish a common goal is a good way to build cohesion in a small team. Normally, such bonding requires a long period of working together to become strong. However, the addition of danger and potential death which can be prevented only by trust and teamwork, plus living together 24 hours a day for days and weeks on end, forges the bond much faster and stronger. Combat soldiers describe the bond, hesitantly or openly, as love.

c.   The closest bonding naturally forms with one's buddy in combat—the only soldier with whom an individual ideally can share his deepest thoughts and concerns. This bonding will also include the other close team members. Some of these may be people whom a person might have expected (and probably did expect on first introduction) to dislike intensely due to individual personality differences or ethnic or racial prejudices. However, once these soldiers have proved themselves reliable, trustworthy, and competent, they become bonded brothers in arms. Being included in the cohesion does have to be earned by combat performance, but once established, it can lead the team to overlook or even condone other noncombat-related faults.

3-8. HORIZONTAL AND VERTICAL BONDING

a.   *An Interlocking Framework.* Horizontal bonding is the personal loyalty between peers in the small team. This must be complemented by vertical bonding (the personal loyalty and trust between the team's enlisted soldiers and their officer and NCO leaders). At the next higher echelon, the junior officers and NCOs must develop strong horizontal bonding with their peers and vertical bonding with their leaders. This hierarchical framework of personal loyalty and trust is needed to provide the troops at the small team level with a transmitted confidence in the units to their right, left, front and rear.

b.   *Cohesion, Operational Readiness Training.* The Army's experimental cohesion, operational readiness training (COHORT) program creates new combat arms companies which keep the same soldiers together through basic training and link them with their leaders in advanced individual training. The COHORT program then keeps the personnel in the company or platoons together (as much as possible) through the first enlistment. This maximizes the horizontal bonding and first level of vertical bonding. Studies have confirmed that CO-HORT companies quickly reach a higher level of proficiency than units with high turnover of personnel (turbulence). They score high on measures of cohesion. However, they also demand much more of their leaders.

c. *Cautions.* Personal bonding is not enough to produce a good military unit. It is possible to have teams which share very high personal bonding, but which are not dedicated to the units' combat mission. In that situation, their cohesiveness may be directed solely to keeping each other comfortable and safe. Such teams can be difficult and even dangerous to lead. They may try to take as little risk as possible, and leaders who lead them into danger, for example, may find themselves alone and unsupported.

3-9. UNIT IDENTITY

a. *Esprit de Corps.* Team cohesion must be strengthened by a sense of the unit's military history and its mission and by a sense of shared identity which reminds soldiers of how they should act. This sense is called esprit de corps or simply esprit.

(1) In ancient Rome this identity was formed around the numbered Legion (such as Julius Caesar's famous Tenth) with its golden eagle standard.

(2) In the British Army, a soldier's identity is still strongly focused on the Regiment, with the unit's hundreds of years of history, and supported usually by a regional basis for recruiting.

(3) Since the Civil War and WWI, the US Army has discouraged regional recruiting. The focus for our military identity has tended to be the branch (with its insignia), special training (airborne or ranger tabs, green or red berets), the division (with its distinctive patch), and the battalion (with its unit flag and battle streamers).

b. *New Manning System.* The Army's new manning system is seeking to reinforce unit identity by designating regiments and giving them distinctive regimental crests. The system will encourage career progression which brings the same officers and NCOs together again in different assignments. This will provide the personnel more time working together in which to form horizontal and vertical bonding at all levels. It also will increase the shared sense of tradition.

c.   *Summary.* The patches, insignias, flags, and standards provide visual reminders of the tradition and quick identifiers of who our fellow members are. The names or numbers which designate the unit provide a conceptual framework for the esprit de corps to develop around. However, the more important issue is the content of the verbal or written tradition. For the esprit de corps to call forth positive combat stress behaviors under stress, it must model the desired behaviors—courage, loyalty to buddies, obedience to all lawful orders, initiative and ingenuity, endurance even in the face of impending disaster, and self-sacrifice. It must also uphold the code of honorable conduct of American values and the Law of Land Warfare.

3-10. UNIT COHESION

a.   Especially in small units, all soldiers come to know and appreciate their peers and leaders. They recognize how all members of the unit depend on one another. With this recognition comes a feeling of intimacy (personal bonding) and a strong sense of responsibility. This mutual trust, based on personal face-to-face interaction, is called "cohesion." Also important is esprit de corps, the feeling of identification and membership in the larger, enduring unit with its history and ideals—the battalion, regiment, and division, and beyond them the branch and the US Army. Cohesion holds units together; esprit keeps them dedicated to the mission. Personal bonding alone is like steel wire mesh: it is extremely hard to break but easy to bend. Unit identity (or patriotism, or other abstract ideals) is like concrete: it keeps its shape but shatters easily under the pressure and pounding of combat. Combining the two is like reinforced concrete: it neither bends nor breaks. It can only be chipped away chip by chip and is extremely hard to demolish even that way.

b.   Like other positive combat stress behaviors, unit cohesion is not free of potential drawbacks. The possible liabilities resulting from an excessive sense of eliteness was mentioned above in paragraph 3-4. Highly cohesive units may also be really slow to accept and incorporate new replacements. When too many of the old unit members are lost in too short a time, the unit may either fail catastrophically, lose many veterans as battle fatigue casualties, or lose the unit esprit and become totally concerned only with self and buddy survival. Unit leaders and the higher headquarters need to take appropriate actions to safeguard against these possibilities.

3-11. HEROISM

a   The ultimate positive combat stress behaviors are acts of heroism. The citations for winners of the Medal of Honor or other awards for valor in battle document almost unbelievable feats of courage, strength, and endurance. The hero has overcome the paralysis of fear, and in some cases, has also called forth muscle strength far beyond what he has ever used before. He many have persevered in spite of wounds which would normally be so painful as to be disabling. Some heroes willingly sacrifice their lives knowingly for the sake of their buddies.

b.   Those who survive their own heroism often have a difficult time describing how it happened. A few may not even remember the events clearly (have amnesia). More often they remember selected details with remarkable clarity. They may say, "I don't know how I did it. I remember being pinned down and scared, but I saw what needed to be done, and something came over me. It was like it was happening to someone else" (or "like I was watching myself in a movie" or "like an out-of-my-body experience").

c.   In psychiatry, these experiences would be called dissociative reactions. If they resulted in inappropriate behavior, they would be classified as dissociative disorders. Indeed, many such cases may go unrecorded except by sad letters from the soldier's commander to the family—killed while performing his duties. However, when the behavior has been directed by sound military training (drill) and strong unit cohesion, the doer receives a well-deserved medal for heroism in order to encourage similar positive combat stress behavior in others. Posthumous medals also console the survivors and the heroes' families and reassure them that the memory of the hero will live on in the unit's tradition. Medals are awarded based on the results of a soldier's actions, not for the motives that prompted such actions or acts of bravery.

3-12. POSITIVE AND MISCONDUCT STRESS BEHAVIORS—
THE DOUBLE-EDGED SWORD

Positive combat stress behaviors and misconduct stress behaviors are to some extent a double-edged sword or two sides of the same coin. The same physiological and psychological processes that result in heroic bravery in one situation can produce criminal acts such as atrocities against enemy prisoners and civilians in another. Stress may drag the sword down in the direction of the misconduct edge, while sound, moral leadership and military training and discipline must direct it upward toward the positive behaviors. (See Figure 3-1.) The following chapters will explore this issue further.

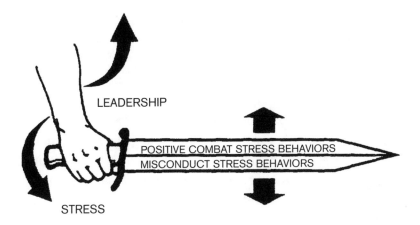

FIGURE 3-1. Positive and misconduct stress behaviors—the double-edged sword.

CHAPTER 4

COMBAT MISCONDUCT STRESS BEHAVIORS

4-1. INTRODUCTION

Misconduct stress behaviors are most likely to occur in units with poor morale or in units where problems exist. This chapter discusses misconduct stress behaviors. It identifies factors which could increase such behaviors and factors which help protect against such behaviors.

4-2. INDICATION OF POTENTIAL MISCONDUCT STRESS BEHAVIORS

Since WWI, leaders and mental health personnel have been taught to monitor for indicators of poor morale and problems in a unit. These indicators may include increased—

- Disease and nonbattle injury rates.
- Disciplinary infractions.
- Absent without leave (AWOL) rates.
- Drug and alcohol abuse.

Often, these misconduct stress behaviors may be the result of stressors and increased stress in a unit. These indicators could be a warning that the potential exists for heavy battle fatigue casualties if this unit is sent to combat.

4-3. BEHAVIORS OF PRIMARY CONCERN TO COMMAND AND THE LAW OF LAND WARFARE

Reacting to some misconduct stress behaviors is primarily the responsibility of the commanders and the legal system. While all misconduct stress behaviors are disciplinary problems, the extreme examples are violations of the Law of Land Warfare. Violations of the Law of Land Warfare must be reported and the offender(s) brought to justice. While medical, psychological, or psychiatric consultation may, in specific cases, be requested to document mental or organic illness that might support a defense of insanity, combat stress alone is no defense for criminal misconduct. Severe combat stress could be considered as an extenuating factor in determining the soldier's sentence. Examples of such misconduct stress behaviors follow.

4-4. THE MISCONDUCT STRESS BEHAVIOR OF OPTING NOT TO TAKE PRISONERS

a.   It has always been true (although not always admitted) that there comes a time in the heat of battle when soldiers in combat may decide to deliberately kill the enemy rather than take them as prisoners. The normal rage of combat stress will not accept that the enemy soldier who has just fought to his last bullet, killed your buddy, and almost killed you should survive to be a prisoner of war (PW), safe from the continuing danger that you must still face. This rage of battle can reach epic proportions in otherwise excellent soldiers. S.L.A. Marshall described two exemplary bayonet assaults in which victorious US units took no prisoners and went on to slaughter the barnyard or pack animals—and were ashamed to admit it afterwards.

b.   Soldiers may feel guilty about not having accepted the surrender of the enemy, just as they often feel guilty about killing their first armed enemy at close range. Later, they may feel guilty about not feeling guilty any more—about how easy it has become.

c.   Good leaders must work to keep the rage of battle from leading to massacre. Appeals to higher ethical ideals and respect for the enemy as brave soldiers similar to ourselves are useful but may be unheeded in the noise of battle. It may be more productive to remind the soldiers (and oneself) that there are good reasons for accepting surrender of the enemy and treating the prisoners humanely:

• Not all the enemy fight to the last bullet. Many probably were there under duress, kept their heads down, and only fired their weapons haphazardly while their superiors were watching.

• Alive, enemy prisoner(s) of war (EPW) may give valuable information to our military intelligence personnel.

• Other enemy soldiers, hearing that surrender is possible, will be less likely to fight so desperately when confronted, thereby decreasing our casualties.

• The enemy will be more likely to accept the surrender of our soldiers who may find themselves in a hopeless position.

• Killing enemy soldiers who are attempting to surrender is murder and a violation of the Law of Land Warfare. It must be reported by any who observe it and may result in trial by court-martial.

• Soldiers who commit such acts in combat are likely to feel great guilt about it after returning home and are often haunted by the memory for the rest of their lives.

4-5. THE MISCONDUCT STRESS BEHAVIOR OF KILLING ENEMY PRISONERS

a.   The ambiguous case of not recognizing attempts to surrender during a hot assault can be distinguished from killing soldiers who surrender after no (or only token) resistance. There is no excuse for killing prisoners after they surrender unless they are resisting or attempting to escape. Although the same urge for revenge may still be understandable, if prisoners are killed without cause, it is undoubtedly murder. Killing of prisoners must be actively prevented by command as a serious violation of the Law of Land Warfare. Violators are subject to trial and punishment.

b.   It is also understandable but an unacceptable stress reaction for stressed commanders to overlook such incidents when done by otherwise good soldiers whom they need as fighters. Overlooking these incidents and failing to take action to prevent them is itself a violation of the Law of Land Warfare and may subject such commanders to trial by court-martial.

NOTE: All personnel, including health care providers and combat stress control/mental health personnel, must be alert for signs of misconduct stress behaviors. They must advise the commander. Chaplains also should be alert and inform command about trends or stories/rumors of misconduct stress behavior. They, however, must maintain an individual soldier's confidentiality if told in the course of their religious duties.

4-6. THE MISCONDUCT STRESS BEHAVIOR OF MUTILATING ENEMY DEAD

a.   This practice has been prohibited by civilized nations as a violation of the Law of Land Warfare but may still be approved in some regions of the world. Collecting scalps, ears, gold teeth, and so forth as trophies can still become common practice (as in the island battles of the Pacific in WWII) as signs of racial hatred and dehumanization against a stubborn and merciless enemy.

b.   Leaving deliberately mutilated bodies (especially with facial and genital mutilation) for the enemy to find is less common, but also occurs as bitterness increases. Despoiling or pillaging the dead is, of course, a war crime and is punishable by court-martial.

NOTE: Mutilating the dead must be prohibited, since it dehumanizes both those who do it and those who condone it. It tends to provoke reprisals, alienate world and home front opinion, and contribute to guilt and post-traumatic stress symptoms when the soldier returns home.

4-7. THE MISCONDUCT STRESS BEHAVIORS OF TORTURING PRISONERS, USING EXCESSIVE FORCE OR BRUTALITY, AND KILLING ANIMALS

a.   In some cultures or religions (such as many of the seventeenth/eighteenth century North American Indian tribes), torture has been accepted by all parties as the proper thing to do. The captive warrior who died bravely under torture was highly respected. Under the Law of Land Warfare, torture is a war crime and is forbidden but is still sometimes practiced. It may be erroneously justified as necessary to gain information to assure victory and save friendly lives or to intimidate the opposition, especially in counterinsurgency scenarios.

NOTE: If torture to gain information or to intimidate is allowed, even tacitly, it can become an all-too-easy outlet for combat stress-related tension and frustration, with steadily worsening consequences.

b.   The more insidious and common form of this misconduct stress behavior is to react with excessive force or brutality to episodes of provocation. The boundary between excessive and prudent is a gray area. It is related to the magnitude of the enemy provocation and the likelihood of its continuing if not answered. Examples of overreaction include reacting to a single sniper or mortar fire from a civilian housing area with massive artillery and air attack, or going in to beat all the villagers and destroy all the houses.

c.   It is difficult and frustrating for soldiers to adhere to strict rules of engagement, such as never firing into civilian areas until fired on and only returning fire with precision when the specific enemy has been located. It is especially difficult if the enemy is deliberately using such areas as sanctuaries and the civilians are tacitly or even explicitly siding with the enemy. Such self-control is, however, often essential to accomplish the national objectives in military operations other than war. To maintain fire discipline, leaders must instill and continually reinforce a sense of strong unit identity and cohesion that actively encourages and rewards correct behavior.

d.   Stress-induced behaviors that impair fire discipline can also cause friendly fire casualties. In some cases, overeagerness to attack the enemy (perhaps resulting from the positive combat stress behaviors of desire for glory, medals, or promotion) may lead to tragic error. Too much arousal or anxiety may cause soldiers who are "on a hair trigger" to misidentify vehicles, to make errors in reading maps or grid coordinates, or to shoot first and ask questions later. There is a well-documented tendency for hypervigilant persons to misinterpret and even to misperceive stimuli in ways which seem to confirm their preconceived fears.

(1) Consider the pressure on the tank crew which is constantly remembering that in an engagement between two equal opponents the tank that fires second has only one chance out of five of surviving. Add to that many hours of continuous operations and rapid movement with little sleep. Now add that beyond the unit's right boundary is an unknown friendly unit. This unit may be from a different division, corps, service, or allied nation. The tank unit's leader and higher headquarters must recognize that these tank crews are at

high risk of violating the TSOP and firing across the boundary into the neighboring area.

(2) In such situations, the unit leaders (even tired, anxious leaders) must perform a recurring process of risk analysis and risk management. Friendly fire casualties cannot rationally be completely prevented in modern, fast-moving battles. Commanders and leaders must implement policies and prudent precautions which will minimize friendly fire casualties while also minimizing the risk of the enemy killing our soldiers.

(3) The targeting policy which maximizes the odds of hitting the enemy first may be entirely justified at the beginning of the battle. Then, the enemy's strength is uncertain and his crews and tanks must be assumed approximately equal in quality to our own. Later in the battle, a more cautious policy may be justified. It may be clearer that most (if not all) of the enemy are undertrained, out-gunned, and badly overstressed. Our own crews, though still aggressive, are becoming fatigued as a result of the battle or because of sleep loss. Their alertness, coordination, and senses may be dull.

(4) The leaders must recognize these stress factors. They must implement precautions to ensure that there are no friendly fire casualties. They must consider modifying or changing the targeting policy if stress factors are high. They must then assure that the change, its reasons, and any related coordinating instructions are passed down the chain of command to every crew. Recent experience is that leaders will be held publicly accountable if they fail to do this and friendly deaths result. This is true even though the leaders' misconduct may be a reaction only to their own combat stress.

e. Other examples of excessive force or brutality involve the killing of animals.

(1) Soldiers may deliberately shoot domestic animal(s) of local farmers as acts of hatred or revenge. Soldiers may later claim that the animal(s)' death was an accident. Leaders should investigate and ensure appropriate actions are implemented to prevent future incidents of this nature. All soldiers must understand that the senseless killing of animals is a punishable crime under the UCMJ.

(2) Warning signs of excessive stress may be indicated when individual soldiers begin to mistreat, torture, and kill animals. These types of behaviors are warning signs to commanders and leaders that self-control among some of their soldiers is wearing thin. Unit cohesion may also suffer, since other members of the unit may feel revulsion and anger at such behaviors. Leadership must recognize such signs of stress and take actions to provide less destructive ways of relieving the tension and frustration.

4-8. THE MISCONDUCT STRESS BEHAVIORS OF LOOTING, PILLAGE, AND RAPE

a.   All these behaviors (looting, pillage, and rape) may be misconduct stress behaviors, although they may also be committed by soldiers with antisocial norms or personality traits and no combat exposure. They may reflect aberrant group norms in soldiers who have experienced little combat stress. Less than 180 years ago, it was the accepted custom that besieged cities which did not surrender before their wall was breached and which therefore had to be taken by assault, were always turned over to the troops to loot and rape. This is no longer acceptable and is a violation of the Law of Land Warfare. However, the stressed combat veteran may still feel entitled to collect souvenirs and perhaps to loot, pillage, and even rape the hostile (or even friendly) noncombatants. He may feel he has earned the right by his suffering, risks, and losses.

b.   Rape is sometimes used as a symbolic act of dominance, not only over female victims, but also over males in her social system who are powerless to prevent it. Rape forcibly degrades and humiliates the victim and everyone in his or her group, which naturally provokes resentment and reprisal.

NOTE: Only a strong chain of command and a unit identity which says, "We don't do that and those who do aren't one of us and will be punished" can keep looting and rape from happening.

c.   The distinction between looting and raping local nationals versus voluntary donation and social interactions is not always clear when only the soldiers have weapons. Sexual exploitation of local women by soldiers may foster local resentment and detract from the mission, even when paid for with food, cigarettes, money, or luxury items. Leaders, combat stress control/mental health personnel, and chaplains need to be alert to these facts to prevent abuse. It is the commander's responsibility to set and demand high standards as the ethical role model for the unit.

4-9. THE MISCONDUCT STRESS BEHAVIOR OF FRATERNIZATION

a.   Incidents of fraternization, sexual favoritism or harassment, prostitution, and even rape may occur within US Army units. The stress of combat, the reminders of the nearness of death, prolonged separation from home, boredom, and other stressors bring out the natural human tendencies to form relationships—or to exercise aggressive impulses and personal dominance.

(1) Sexual misconduct stress behaviors within units can be destructive to unit cohesion and morale. That is especially true when leader-subordinate or officer-enlisted relationships are (or are misperceived to be) directly involved. Even misconduct stress behaviors involving mutually consenting peers can seriously disrupt unit functioning. This can also hamper individual and family readjustment after the return home.

(2) All unit members, as well as unit leaders and staff members of higher commands, have the personal responsibly to maintain a professional and social climate which prevents the misconduct of fraternization from getting started. Everyone should actively discourage (rather than tacitly condone or assist) mixed-gender couples from pairing off except when required by the mission. At the same time, there should be ample opportunity for larger group, mixed gender social activities and morale support.

b.   Leadership must set the example and must enforce the UCMJ regulations against fraternization, harassment, adultery, and criminal assault. The enforcement policy must be made unquestionably clear to all unit members in advance. Punishment for violating the fraternization policy must be evenly and strictly executed.

4-10. THE MISCONDUCT STRESS BEHAVIOR OF KILLING NONCOMBATANTS

a.　Some incidents of mass execution of civilians (for example, those committed by Nazi Germany) are acts of deliberate policy and are outside the scope of this discussion. Others, like the My Lai massacre in Vietnam, although premeditated, are clearly reactions to cumulative combat stress. These misconduct stress behaviors are likely, especially in guerrilla warfare, when some seemingly noncombatants, such as women and children, are in fact ununiformed combatants. Misconduct stress behavior is also likely when the sympathies of the civilian noncombatants have become suspect as they allow the soldiers' buddies to be killed and mutilated by mines and booby traps which they themselves avoid.

b.　Other examples of killing civilians may be impulsive, individual stress reactions or rage attacks: One soldier who has just seen his buddy killed impulsively shoots two children on a water buffalo. The hot, angry, frustrated soldier shoots the peasant who is shouting at him in a foreign language about trampling her vegetable garden. The fact is that overstressed human beings with loaded weapons are inherently dangerous.

NOTE: Commission of murder and other atrocities against noncombatants must be reported as a war crime and punished if responsibility is established. This must be done even though we may pity the overstressed soldier as well as the victims.

4-11. THE MISCONDUCT STRESS BEHAVIOR OF FIGHTING WITH ALLIES OR UNITED STATES FORCES

a.　Fighting is, of course, what soldiers are trained to do, but they are supposed to direct that skill and energy against the enemy. However, highly cohesive groups, where they believe they are the best, naturally make derogatory remarks about each other. Honor may then require that the insult be resolved by fighting. As long as the fighting is fair and forbids dangerous weapons and crippling techniques, it may actually help sustain cohesion and fighting spirit while promoting grudgingly mutual respect. Such fights between members of different units with rival traditions, different services, or allied forces have sometimes been tacitly or even explicitly condoned by their leaders. A better solution is to initiate a competitive sports program among the rivals which allows them to test each other's strength and courage with less risk of serious injury.

b.   Fighting against allies and other US forces becomes a more dangerous stress behavior when it is the result of—

- Alcohol abuse.
- Stress of impending or past battle.
- Battle-generated mistrust.
- Cultural differences.
- Racial prejudice.
- Ethnic prejudice.

It clearly becomes misconduct when the rules of fairness are stretched so that seriously harmful tactics, techniques, and weapons are used. The result is then injury or death. Persistent bad feelings may result that interfere with cooperation between units, services, and allies.

c.   This misconduct stress behavior is most common in the period of tension before deployment to battle, or of persistent tension during prolonged lulls or withdrawal of units from combat. Most soldiers who are in battle against the real enemy (or on brief R&R) are not looking for these "intramural" fights. However, some rear area support troops may be, to try to enhance their macho image. That can irritate the combat troops until serious fights result.

NOTE: Leaders and combat stress control/mental health personnel must be alert and sensitive to signs that stress is driving high spirits and unit pride across the very fine line from occasional friendly intramural fighting to misconduct stress behaviors.

d.   It is obviously serious when fights break out between groups who have been traditional allies in such brawls, or within a previously cohesive unit. It is also traditionally more serious (and usually subject to serious UCMJ disciplinary action) when a soldier strikes a superior officer or an NCO. This, too, can clearly be due to combat or other stress, which might be taken into consideration in deciding punishment.

4-12. THE MISCONDUCT STRESS BEHAVIOR OF BEING ABSENT WITHOUT LEAVE OR DESERTING

Going AWOL or deserting may be misconduct stress behaviors, but are punishable under the UCMJ unless there exists some legal justification or excuse. Possible defenses to a charge of AWOL or desertion include insanity or amnesia with the (rare) trance type of battle fatigue. In the Western democracies, less use of capital punishment for civilian crimes has also reduced the frequency of firing-squad executions of deserters "to discourage the others." Nevertheless, the death penalty is still allowed under the UCMJ for deserting in time of war.

4-13. THE MISCONDUCT STRESS BEHAVIOR OF REFUSING TO OBEY AN ORDER

a. A soldier deliberately refusing to obey an order in combat, as a misconduct stress behavior, may be tactically inappropriate (based on an unduly narrow, self-interested, or pessimistic perception of the situation). Alternatively, it may be tactically appropriate (based on a realistic perception that the order is unwise and will get one killed for no purpose). However, all orders which do not involve explicit violation of the Law of Land Warfare are presumed to be lawful and must be obeyed. The dictates of a person's conscience, religion, or personal philosophy (let alone fear or misgivings) cannot legally justify or excuse the disobedience of a lawful order. Combat refusal by units has historically been dealt with by measures as extreme as summary execution of ringleaders or decimation (the arbitrary execution of every tenth soldier). The UCMJ currently provides a maximum punishment of death for this offense when it is committed before the enemy.

b. Army operations expects leaders to keep troops informed of the "Big Picture" and the commanders' intent. Good leaders may give their subordinates more opportunity to express their concerns about an order which they consider unwise and to suggest alternatives to accomplish the objective. Once ordered, however, combat refusal of lawful orders will still be punishable. The alternatives to unwise yet lawful orders will continue to be—

• An appeal to higher headquarters through the chain of command, chain of support, or special staff (perhaps with a dramatic demonstration of good faith, such as requesting to be relieved of responsibility or command while continuing in the mission as a common soldier).

• Vigorous compliance to the lawful order (it is worth remembering that the famous Charge of the Light Brigade in the Crimean War was successful, although costly and pointless except for the glory it won).

• Cautious and skillful compliance while hoping for a reappraisal and reprieve.

• Unacceptable solutions, such as one of the other negative combat stress behaviors, including involuntary disability through battle fatigue.

c. Less extreme forms of this type of misconduct stress behaviors would be refusing, ignoring, shirking, or otherwise avoiding orders which do not involve the combat mission. The orders may be obeyed but with obvious signs of disrespect to the superior officer or NCO. Persistent breaches of military courtesies, uniform regulations, and other general orders or TSOPs may also be misconduct stress behaviors and are sometimes seen in otherwise effective combat veterans.

d. The distinction between misconduct stress behavior and battle fatigue can be blurred in reality. If an act of insubordination is clearly a misconduct stress behavior and the tactical situation allows, the leader may elect to handle it by telling everyone, "Oh, he's just got battle fatigue" and treating it with reassurance, brief rest, physical replenishment, and activities to restore confidence. In a situation that requires stronger disciplinary action, such as insolence or assault on a superior, the soldier may be charged with insubordination or combat refusal even though it is a misconduct stress behavior.

4-14. THE MISCONDUCT STRESS BEHAVIOR OF THREATENING TO KILL OR KILLING UNIT LEADERS OR OTHER SOLDIERS

a. Threatening to kill or killing unpopular leaders or soldiers (called "fragging" and so named from the technique of rolling a fragmentation grenade into the victim's bunker) is also a criminal act and subjects the offender to disciplinary action. To the extent that this behavior is related to combat stress (rather than to some other grudge), it may involve an individual or group perception that the victim is—

- Excessively eager to commit the unit to danger.
- Grossly incompetent.
- Unfair in sharing of the risks.

b.   Other cases may be unpremeditated flashes of rage provoked by intense stress and the loss of usual inhibitions against violence through combat experience. For example, a special operations forces medic had just brought his dead teammate from an ambush to a supporting hospital. When a mortuary affairs specialist casually flicked cigarette ashes onto his dead buddy's face, the medic drew his knife with every intention of cutting the clerk's head off. Fortunately for both soldiers, bystanders intervened before the clerk was seriously hurt. Fortunately for the medic, his own chain of command understood his misconduct stress behavior. They convinced the hospital commander that it was not in anyone's best interest to press charges.

4-15. MISCONDUCT STRESS BEHAVIORS OF SPECIAL CONCERN TO THE MEDICAL SYSTEM (ALONG WITH COMMAND)

Some soldiers exhibiting misconduct stress behaviors attempt to use the medical evacuation and treatment system to escape their stressful duty. Other soldiers displaying misconduct stress behaviors require medical or surgical treatment for the consequences of their misbehavior. Medical personnel and administrators must recognize these cases and report them to the chain of command. The chain of command may take disciplinary action and act to prevent future cases. These misconduct stress behaviors of special concern are discussed in the following paragraphs.

4-16. MALINGERERS

a.   Malingerers are those few soldiers who, in an effort to avoid duty, deliberately and willfully fake illness, physical disablement, mental lapse, or derangement, including battle fatigue. They must be counseled and returned to their units, even if they are suffering from combat stress. Malingering is an offense under the UCMJ (Article 115). The issue is not the presence of stress but whether the symptoms are under voluntary control. The most reliable test is whether the symptoms go away when the soldier does not think he is being watched and return when he thinks he is. Usually the malingerer cannot fake perfectly the physical and mental indications of true physical or psychiatric disorders.

b.   The problem is how to distinguish malingering from the physical dysfunction, memory loss, and excessive pain and disability forms of battle fatigue (see Chapter 5). Unlike malingering, these are involuntary, but they also may fluctuate over time and with level of attention. They seldom mimic true physical or psychiatric disorders faithfully. It has been observed that the malingerer is likely to resent, avoid, or try to fake diagnostic tests such as hypnosis and truth serum (sodium amytal) interviews. True battle fatigue cases usually cooperate willingly. However, as true battle fatigue cases recover from the psychologically caused loss of physical function, they may go through a phase of feeling that it is now under voluntary control and, feeling guilty, may mistakenly believe (and confess) that they were malingering all along.

c.   The boundary between malingering as a misconduct stress behavior and battle fatigue can be another gray area when both may be present in the same soldier. If all that is needed to correct the apparent deliberate faking and turn the highly stressed malingerer back into a good soldier is a day or two of relatively light duty, physical replenishment, and encouragement, the leader or treater may elect to call it battle fatigue, treat the battle fatigue, and not press charges unless the soldier continues to malinger.

d.   Another form of malingering is making suicide threats and gestures (nonlethal attempts) for the purpose of escaping unwanted duty. Here, the problem is to distinguish malingering from true depression or impaired impulse control due to stress or battle fatigue where the risk of death on a further suicide attempt is very real. Treating the threat or gesture as a cry for help and assisting the soldier in coping with the stressors without sending him home may separate the malingerer from the true sufferer.

4-17. SELF-INFLICTED WOUNDS

a.   Self-inflicted injuries must be investigated. If deliberate, they are a form of malingering under UCMJ (Article 115). Such injuries may require disciplinary action as well as surgical treatment. Typical examples are shooting or stabbing oneself in the foot or nondominant hand. More ingenious is throwing a hand grenade through a door and holding one's arm out in hopes of being hit by a fragment. In WWI, some soldiers deliberately exposed a patch of skin in mustard-contaminated areas. Good and even excellent soldiers have said that the temptation to give oneself a "millon-dollar wound" becomes hard to set aside as the combat stress level increases. Some soldiers yield to the temptation. Occasionally, buddies even collaborate to give each other wounds and alibis. Fatigue, inattention, and carelessness make unintentional self-inflicted wounds more likely.

b.   Preventable DNBI may be the consequences of the inattention and indifference to hygiene and self-care. Inattention and indifference are common signs of battle fatigue. The results of stress-induced negligence may include dehydration, diarrhea, dysentery, malaria, blisters, and cold injury. Also, stress-induced carelessness can cause mashed fingers, sprained ankles, and more serious bodily injuries. Such disabling conditions may be a deliberate form of malingering; however, this is often difficult to prove. Sex with promiscuous partners and prostitutes may result in sexually transmitted diseases (STD). With the spread of acquired immunodeficiency syndrome (AIDS), STD can once again result in a soldier's slow death from a nonbattle cause. All DNBI must be treated and, if necessary, evacuated, but command must be advised to redouble self-aid, buddy aid, and preventive medicine measures. If these actions are not done, a few negligent cases can quickly grow into an epidemic or an evacuation syndrome. Examples include gonorrhea (WWII Italian theater), frostbite (Korea), and malaria (Vietnam).

c.   Other equally important considerations are wounds or death due to failure to take cover or other obvious precautions. While this is not deliberate misconduct, there are many anecdotes of combat-experienced soldiers who reach a stage where they appear to be functioning well but are so task-oriented or so fatalistic that they become easy, unnecessary victims. Many such cases involved leaders who failed to take cover in the presence of known snipers. Some survived to require surgical care. Many did not. It seems that the psychological defense mechanisms of the resistance stage of stress have betrayed, rather than protected, them. In other cases, inattention due to fatigue played an important role. In a few cases where other background data are available, unconscious or deliberate suicidal intent may be suspected.

4-18. DRUG AND ALCOHOL ABUSE

a.   Substance abuse is classified as a neuropsychiatric disorder, but may also be misconduct stress behavior. It may represent self-medication for the anxiety and traumatic memories of combat or for the boredom and frustrations of rear area duties. Substance abuse may give group users an extended family and an inappropriate sense of belonging to a special group who is "superior" to (but persecuted by) outsiders or authority. This may be an unfortunate by-product of cohesion-producing group dynamics.

b.   The following are some of the problems related to substance abuse:

• Intoxication or withdrawal (from alcohol, barbiturates, tranquilizers, narcotics, stimulants, and hallucinogenic drugs) may require hospitalization for medical/neuropsychiatric stabilization.

• Overuse of amphetamine-type stimulants (as deliberate abuse or by well-intentioned soldiers and leaders trying to stay alert) may cause panic attacks, manic hyperactivity, rage attacks, and paranoid psychosis. Discontinuing amphetamines causes a "crash" with possible serious depression and suicidal thinking.

• Abuse of anabolic steroids for body-building has been associated with mood swings and violent attack episodes ("roid rage").

• Hallucinogenic drugs cause bizarre sensory distortion, poor judgment, and occasionally, panic and dangerous behavior. Fumes (inhaled accidentally or as deliberate abuse) from gasoline, solvents, and spray can propellants can cause disoriented, crazy, and violent behavior.

• Atropine, the antidote for nerve agents, can cause severe heat stress, as well as vision and cognitive problems, even at low doses. Higher doses may produce disoriented, crazy behavior if administered when no nerve agent is present. This is especially true in sleep-deprived or otherwise physiologically overstressed soldiers.

c.   Substance dependency and addiction require rehabilitation or administrative disposition. Some substance abusers have good potential for return to duty, especially if the use is stress-related. It is important not to reward substance abuse with medical evacuation to CONUS unless there are other medical or surgical complications which require it. Detoxication should be accomplished in the theater (combat zone or COMMZ) and the soldier returned to duty for administrative action.

4-19. FACTORS WHICH INCREASE MISCONDUCT STRESS BEHAVIOR

The following factors may increase misconduct stress behavior:

a.   Permissive attitude and availability and use of drugs in the region by civilians, especially around posts or garrison areas.

b.   Inadequate enforcement of the unit's Alcohol and Drug Abuse Prevention and Control Program before deployment; failing to identify and treat (or discharge) misusers. This is a critical issue for Reserve Component as well as Active Component units.

c.   Availability and distribution networks (both legal and illegal) for alcohol and different types of drugs in the theater. Some drugs are much more available at lower prices in some foreign countries or regions.

d.   Unsupervised and unwise use of amphetamines and other strong stimulants to remain awake in CONOPS. This can produce dangerous (usually temporary) neuropsychiatric illness. Also, it may lead to dependency and addiction in originally well-intentioned, good soldiers, including leaders.

e.   Boredom and monotonous duties, especially if combined with chronic frustration and tension.

f.   False alarms of nerve agent presence resulting in self-administration of atropine. Atropine can cause problems with vision, cognitive skills, and performance if taken when a nerve agent is not present.

g.   Victorious pursuit of a retreating enemy. This reduces battle fatigue casualties but may not inhibit commission of criminal acts (killing of EPW, rape, looting) or alcohol/drug misuse unless command retains tight moral control.

h.   Hasty withdrawal. Here, few battle fatigue casualties enter medical channels, although battle fatigue soldiers may be lost as KIA, missing in action (MIA), or captured instead of becoming medical patients. Other stressed soldiers may willfully desert or surrender. Looting can occur, "justified" by the rationalization that the property would just be seized by the enemy. Rape, murder, and other criminal actions taken as reprisal can be triggered by stress if the retreating troops feel hindered by EPW or if the civilians being left behind were not friendly. Leaders must take care not to lose control of the withdrawal or be too zealous in encouraging a "scorched earth" policy.

i.   Beleaguered unit which cannot evacuate any (or only the most severely wounded) casualties. Here, too, few soldiers are identified as battle fatigue casualties although some may become ineffective due to the severe stress. Other soldiers may go AWOL.

j.   Rapid return of soldiers to close contact with noncombatant military, civilians, or families after an intense battle experience without a unit stand-down period in which to defuse.

k.   Commission of atrocities by the enemy, especially if against US personnel, but also if against local civilians.

l.   Racial and ethnic tension which can occur within the US civilian population and among Army personnel. Tension and misconduct may also stem from major cultural and physical/racial differences between US soldiers and the local population.

m.   Local civilian population may be perceived as hostile, untrustworthy, or "subhuman." This is more likely to happen if there is a lack of education and understanding of cultural differences. Exploitation of cultural differences through propaganda to create disharmony and mistrust may be an objective of the enemy.

n.   Failure of expected support, such as reinforcement or relief; inadequate resupply; inadequate medical support and evacuation. Soldiers who feel abandoned and on their own may resort to illegal measures to get what they think they need. Combat soldiers naturally tend to feel "entitled" to claim what they have "earned," and this may lead to looting and worse.

o.   High personnel turbulence, lack of unit cohesion, especially of vertical bonding between leaders and troops. Substance-of-choice" can become a "ticket" for inclusion into a group.

p.   Loss of confidence in leaders, in supporting or allied units, and in equipment as compared to the enemy's. These also can lead soldiers to a sense of abandonment, desperation, and the "right" to take shortcuts to get what they need and deserve.

q.   Popular opposition at home to the war; lack of understanding or belief in the justness of the effort. Some soldiers may find this an excuse to desert or refuse lawful orders. Others who continue to do their duty may show their resentment by lashing out at the local population or by using drugs and alcohol.

r.   Lack of a believable plan for protecting families in the theater, either by evacuating them or keeping them secure under reliable authority. Some soldiers may go AWOL to stay with them or attempt to take them to safety.

4-20. FACTORS WHICH PROTECT AGAINST MISCONDUCT STRESS BEHAVIOR

a.   The following factors protect against misconduct stress behaviors:

• High unit cohesion—represents the commitment of soldiers of all ranks to each other and the strength of their willingness to fight and sacrifice personal safety. It is a product of bonding of soldiers with each other and the bonding between leaders and subordinates. Cohesion requires strong bonds of mutual respect, trust, confidence, and understanding within units. Cohesive units function smoothly and perform well under stress. In organizations with high cohesion, the unit identity forbids abuse of substances and emphasizes adherence to the Law of Land Warfare.

• Tough, realistic training—provides the training, including faithful adherence to rules of engagement, which support the Law of Land Warfare and addresses cultural issues. Tough and realistic training is designed to develop and challenge each soldier and unit. Tough training occurs when leaders and soldiers mutually experience realistic exhausting conditions that prepare both, as a team, for the stress of combat.

• Unit leaders, medical personnel, and chaplains are trained— to recognize battle fatigue and early warning signs of misconduct stress behaviors.

• Units are withdrawn from combat periodically—to rest, refit (reconstitute if necessary), and absorb new replacements who arrive and are integrated as cohesive teams, not individuals.

• Leaders demonstrate competence, courage, candor, and commitment. Leaders show caring for the soldiers and make provisions for their physical, mental, and spiritual well-being as the tactical situation permits.

• Leaders keep troops informed—of the objectives of the operations and war (including psychological operations and diplomatic, political, and moral objectives). They focus the soldiers' appraisal of the situation to maintain positive coping against the temptations to misconduct stress behaviors. The commander should utilize his public affairs officer and the public affairs assistance available to him in an effort to keep soldiers informed.

• Leaders conduct after-action debriefings—which defuse resentments and tension prior to soldiers coming in close contact with noncombatants (miliary, allied, civilian, or family). This is most important for soldiers who return from special operations, direct action, special reconnaissance, or counterterrorism missions.

b.   The situations listed above can be extremely beneficial for leaders and troops in maintaining and enforcing a unit self-image that regards misconduct behaviors as unacceptable. If that view is lacking, these same situations may even contribute to substance abuse and violations of the laws of war.

CHAPTER 5

BATTLE FATIGUE

5-1. INTRODUCTION

Battle fatigue is the approved US Army term (AR 40-216) for combat stress symptoms and reactions which—

• Feel unpleasant.

• Interfere with mission performance.

• Are best treated with reassurance, rest, replenishment of physical needs, and activities which restore confidence.

a. Battle fatigue can also be present in soldiers who have been physically wounded or who have nonbattle injuries or diseases caused by stressors in the combat area. It may be necessary to treat both the battle fatigue and the other problems.

b. Battle fatigue may coexist with misconduct stress behaviors. However, battle fatigue itself, by definition, does not warrant legal or disciplinary action.

c. Several of our allies use other terms for battle fatigue such as combat reaction, combat stress reaction, or battle shock.

5-2. CONTRIBUTING FACTORS WHICH CAUSE BATTLE FATIGUE

There are four major contributing factors which cause battle fatigue. They are—

• Sudden exposure.

• Cumulative exposure.

• Physical stressors and stress symptoms.

• Home front and other existing problems.

Any one factor may suffice if intense enough. Usually two, three, or all four factors can collectively produce battle fatigue.

a.   The first factor is the sudden exposure or transition to the intense fear, shocking stimuli, and life-and-death consequences of battle. This occurs most commonly when soldiers are committed to battle the first time but can happen even to veteran soldiers when they come under sudden, intense attack. Soldiers in "safe" rear areas may be overwhelmed by the horrible stimuli and consequences of war without themselves being under fire. This is an occupational hazard for rearward command and support personnel, including medical.

b.   The second factor is the cumulative exposure to dangers, responsibilities, and horrible consequences. Exposure can cause repeated grief and guilt over loss of fellow soldiers. It can also give the sense that one's own luck, skill, and courage have been used up. The rate of accumulation depends on the rate of losses (KIA, WIA, died of wounds [DOW], and other causes) and of "close calls" with disaster and death (including being wounded oneself). Periods of rest, recreation, and retraining in which new supportive, cohesive bonds are formed may temporarily reverse the accumulation but not stop it completely.

c.   The third factor is the physical stressors and stress symptoms which reduce coping ability. Sleep loss and dehydration are especially strong contributors. Also important are physical overwork, cold, heat, wetness, noise, vibration, blast, fumes, lack of oxygen, chronic discomfort, poor hygiene, disrupted nutrition, low-grade fevers, infections, and other environmental illnesses. These stressors are also in the area of responsibility of preventive medicine. In moderate amounts, such physical stressors contribute to battle fatigue but are reversed by rest and time for restoration. In higher doses, they cause serious illness or injury requiring specific medical or surgical treatment. When the major contributing factors to battle fatigue are physical stresses that can be reversed, treatment is usually simple and recovery is rapid. However, physical factors are not necessarily the cause of battle fatigue. When the soldier is diagnosed, the absence of obvious physical stressors should not detract from the positive expectation of rapid and full recovery.

d.   The fourth factor is the home front and preexisting problems.

(1) Israeli studies found that the strongest factor which distinguished between soldiers who were decorated for heroic acts and

those who became battle shock casualties was having had many recent changes on the home front. The negative home front problem may be a "Dear John" letter, a sick parent or child, or bad debts. Or it may be something positive—being recently married or becoming a parent. Worrying about what is happening back home distracts soldiers from focusing their psychological defenses on the combat stressors. It creates internal conflict between performing their combat duty and perhaps resolving the home front problems or concerns.

(2) The second strongest factor found in the Israeli studies was unit cohesion: the soldiers who became stress casualties were often committed to battle alongside strangers, while those who became heroes were alongside unit members they knew well, trusted, and depended on. These findings confirm observations from previous wars. Other baseline stressors which are often cited include lack of information; lack of confidence in leaders, supporting units, or equipment in comparison with the enemy's; and lack of belief in the justness of the war (which may reflect lack of support for the effort in the US).

(3) It is worth noting that individual personality makeup does not predict susceptibility to battle fatigue. Careful studies by the US Army after WWII and by the Israelis since the Yom Kippur War all show that there is no clear relationship between neurotic traits or personality disorders and battle fatigue. People with these traits were no more likely to become battle fatigue casualties and no less likely to be decorated for valor than were those soldiers who tested as normal.

(4) There are personality factors which may predict who will be poor soldiers (or who may be prone to commit acts of misconduct if given opportunities or excuses to) but not who will get battle fatigue. There are good predictors of battle fatigue but individual personalty type is not one of them. Anyone may become a battle fatigue casualty if too many high-risk factors occur. However, personality factors may help predict who is less likely to recover quickly after being disabled by battle fatigue.

e.   There are two common themes which interact in varying combinations in most battle fatigue casualties—loss of confidence and internal conflict of motives.

(1) Battle-fatigued soldiers have often lost confidence in—

• Themselves—their own strength, alertness, and abilities, or the adequacy of their training.

• Equipment—their weapons and the supporting arms.

• Buddies—other members of the small unit, or in the reliability of supporting units.

• Leaders, to include—

• The skill and competence of the small unit leader or the senior leadership.

• Whether the leaders care about the soldiers' well-being and survival.

• The leader's candor (honesty) or courage.

These doubts plus the soldiers' estimate of the threat situation, raise questions about their chances of surviving and/or of succeeding with the mission. Loss of faith in whether the "cause" is worth suffering and dying for also plays a role. It has been said that soldiers join the military services for patriotism, but they fight and die for their buddies and trusted leaders. Soldiers do not want their comrades or themselves to die for an unjust cause or for others' mistakes. Loss of faith may even spread to a painful loss of belief in the goodness of life and other spiritual and religious values.

(2) Combat, by its nature, creates conflicts between motives within an individual. The desire for survival and comfort is in conflict with the fears of failure or disgrace and the soldier's loyalty to buddies. Leaders' actions must—

• Raise the soldier's confidence.

• Help resolve the soldier's internal conflict in favor of his sense of duty.

5-3. SIGNS/SYMPTOMS OF BATTLE FATIGUE

a.   *Simple Fatigue.* The simple fatigue or exhaustion form of battle fatigue is normally the most common. It involves tiredness, loss of initiative, indecisiveness, inattention, and, when extreme, general apathy. These cases may show some features of the other forms, especially anxiety and pessimism, but not to the degree that they cannot rest and recover in their own unit (duty) or in a nonmedical support unit (rest). However, the tactical situation may call for them to rest in medical cots if no other suitable place is practical.

b.   *Anxious.* The anxious form is naturally one of the most common, given the danger of combat. Symptoms include verbal expressions of fear; marked startle responses which cease to be specific to true threat stimuli and become generalized; tremor; sweating; rapid heartbeat; insomnia with terror dreams, and other symptoms of hyperarousal. This form is often seen while the soldier is close to the danger and shifts to the exhausted or depressed form as he is evacuated towards the rear.

c.   *Depressed.* The depressed form is also common. It may have the slowed speech and movement of the simple fatigue form or the restlessness and startle responses of the anxious form. The depressed form also has significant elements of self-doubt, self-blame, hopelessness, and may include grief and bereavement. The soldier may be pessimistic about the chance for victory or survival. The self-blame and guilt may be about perceived or actual failures in the combat role or mistakes made. It may be related to home front issues. Or it may be relatively pure survivor guilt—the irrational feeling of a survivor that he should have died with members of his unit or in place of a buddy.

d.   *Memory Loss.* The memory loss form is usually less common, especially in its extreme versions. Mild forms include inability to remember recent orders and instructions. More serious examples are loss of memory for well-learned skills or discrete loss of memory for an especially traumatic event or period of time. Extreme forms include disorientation and regression to a precombat (for example, childhood) state. Total amnesia, or a fugue state in which the soldier leaves the threatening situation altogether, forgets his own past, and is found wandering somewhere else (having taken on another superficial identity), can also occur. Physical causes of amnesia such as concussion or substance misuse (for example, alcohol) must be ruled out in such cases.

e.   *Physical Function Disturbance.* Disturbance of physical function includes disruptions of motor, sensory, and speech functions. Physical injuries or causes are absent or insufficient to explain the symptoms.

- Motor disturbance includes—
  - Weakness or paralysis of hands, limbs, or body.
  - Sustained contractions of muscles (for example, being unable to straighten up or to straighten out the elbow).
  - Gross tremors; pseudoconvulsive seizures (sometimes with loss of consciousness).
- Visual symptoms may include—
  - Blurred or double vision.
  - Tunnel vision.
  - Total blindness.
- Auditory symptoms may involve—
  - Ringing (or other noises) in the ears.
  - Deafness.
  - Dizziness.
- Tactile (skin) sensory changes include—
  - Loss of sensations (anesthesia).
  - Abnormal sensations, such as "pins and needles" (paresthesia).
- Speech disturbance may involve—
  - Stuttering.
  - Hoarseness.
  - Muteness.

(1) The physical symptoms often begin as normal but transitory incoordination, speech difficulties, or sensory disruption. These symptoms are triggered by physical events, such as explosions, mild concussion, or simple fatigue. They are magnified when emotions cannot be expressed because of social pressure or heroic self-image. They are, therefore, most often seen in the "elite" units or groups who show few other cases of battle fatigue, such as officers or the airborne and rangers in WWII. They are also more common in individuals from social classes and cultures that receive less education and/or do not learn how to express feelings in words.

(2) In some cases, the physical "disability" may have a clear symbolic relationship to the specific emotional trauma or conflict of

motivation which the soldier has experienced. The disability may make the soldier unable to do his job and so relieve him from danger, such as classic "trigger-finger palsy." The symptoms may be reinforced by reducing his anxiety and eliminating internal conflict of combat duties. Symptoms also may be reinforced by receiving the relative luxury of rear area food, hygiene, and sleep. However, not all cases fit that pattern. Some soldiers with significant loss of function from battle fatigue have continued to perform their missions under great danger. Medical personnel must be alert to new physical forms of battle fatigue which mimic physical injury, such as might be attributed to lasers, radiation, or chemical agents.

    f. *Psychosomatic Forms.* These psychosomatic forms of battle fatigue commonly present with physical (rather than emotional) symptoms due to stress. These include—

- Cardiorespiratory—
  - Rapid or irregular heartbeat.
  - Shortness of breath.
  - Light-headed.
  - Tingling and cramping of toes, fingers, and lips.
- Gastrointestinal—
  - Stomach pain.
  - Indigestion.
  - Nausea/vomiting.
  - Diarrhea.
- Musculoskeletal—
  - Back or joint pain.
  - Excessive pain and disability from minor or healed wounds.
  - Headache.

According to some WWII battalion surgeons, the psychosomatic form of battle fatigue was the most common form seen at battalion level. This type of case may have accounted for a large percentage of all patients seen at battalion aid stations (BASs) during times of heavy fighting.

    g. *Disruptive Forms.* Disruptive forms of battle fatigue include disorganized, bizarre, impulsive or violent behavior, total withdrawal, or persistent hallucinations. These are uncommon forms of battle fatigue, but they do occur. Battle fatigue symptoms are a nonverbal way for soldiers to communicate to comrades and leaders that they have had all they can stand at the moment. Battle fatigue takes on whatever form the soldiers expect. It is important, therefore, to create positive expectancies and to eliminate the belief that battle fatigue soldiers usually do crazy, senseless, or violent things. Leaders, medics, and combat stress control personnel must ensure that battle fatigue casualties are never referred to as psychiatric casualties.

5-4. LABELING OF BATTLE FATIGUE CASES

a. As stated earlier, battle fatigue is the US Army approved label for this condition. Fatigue implies that it is a normal condition which can occur in anyone who is subjected to the extreme mental and emotional work of combat missions. Fatigue also implies that it gets better quickly with rest. The term should be applied to the normal but uncomfortable reactions to combat stress. It should also be used with the more seriously impairing responses in order that it not take on the connotations of breakdown or a release from duty. However, some cases do require treatment in medical facilities, skilled counseling, and even brief tranquilizing or sedative medication.

b. Historical experience proves that it is important not to try to make early distinctions among battle fatigue cases based on presumed causes and likely response to treatment. Cases due to acute emotional stress versus subacute physical stress versus chronic cumulative stress may need somewhat different treatment. These cases have, on the average, different likelihood for successful return to duty. However, these battle fatigue cases may be quite impossible to distinguish at first by their appearance and symptoms. Accurate individual history may be unattainable during battle and especially during the first interviews. All cases should, therefore, be called battle fatigue and be treated immediately with positive expectation of rapid, full recovery, as close to their units as the tactical situation permits. It is essential to avoid dramatic or medical/psychiatric labels for this condition.

★   ★   ★

CAUTION

Do not prejudge whether a battle fatigue soldier will recover quickly or slowly based on initial appearance. The symptoms are very changeable. Do not rely on initial information about the relative contributions of acute emotional stress, physical fatigue, chronic exposure, or baseline factors. The incomplete history may be misleading.

★   ★   ★

(1) Consider each contributing factor in designing treatment.

    (a) How to reassure.

    (b) How much rest.

    (c) What to replenish first and most.

    (d) What activities to assign to restore confidence.

(2) Keep positive expectation for recovery.

(3) Get more validated information from the rested soldier and the unit.

(4) Revise the plan based on response to treatment.

c. Battle fatigue may occur in anticipation of the action, during the action, or after the action (during lulls when sick call is again possible or when the unit returns to a safe rear area). Usually, the rise in battle fatigue casualties is preceded by 1 to 3 days of increases in the number of soldiers wounded and killed. All of these cases are still called "battle fatigue" as long as the soldiers are in the theater of operations and are expected to recover and return to duty. The terms *conflict fatigue, crisis fatigue, stress fatigue,* or *field fatigue* may be used for peacetime cases which are reactions to intense mission stressors but do not involve actual battle or life-and-death consequences. These cases should be treated the same way as battle fatigue with no negative connotations.

d. Sublabeling of battle fatigue cases is based solely on where they can be treated. Hence, sublabels depend as much on the situation of the unit as on the symptoms shown by the soldier. The labels *light and heavy, duty and rest, hold and refer*, when added to the label *battle fatigue*, are nothing more than a short-hand or brevity code for saying where the soldier is being treated or sent. They have no other meaning and only transient significance. The sublabel should be updated as the soldier improves or arrives at a new echelon of care.

e.   Figure 5-1 diagrams the choices that lead to the several sublabels for battle fatigue cases.

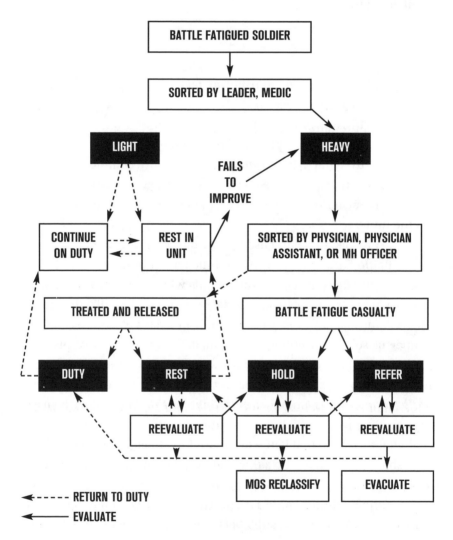

FIGURE 5-1. Diagram of sorting choices and labels for battle fatigue cases.

(1) Light battle fatigue can be managed by self and buddy aid, unit medics, and leader actions. Most soldiers in combat will have light battle fatigue at some time. This includes the normal/common signs of battle fatigue listed in the Graphic Training Aid (GTA) 21-3-4 (available from US Army Training Audiovisual Support Centers). Light battle fatigue also includes the warning (or more serious) signs listed in GTA 21-3-5, provided the signs respond quickly to helping actions. Soldiers with these symptoms do not need to be sent immediately for medical evaluation and can continue on duty. If the symptoms persist after rest, they should be sent to their unit surgeon or physician assistant at routine sick call as heavy.

(2) Heavy battle fatigue (previously called severe) deserves immediate medical evaluation at a medical treatment facility. The symptoms may be—
  • Temporarily too disruptive to the unit's mission.
  • A medical/surgical condition which requires observation and diagnosis to rule out the necessity for emergency treatment. The medical triager sorts the heavy battle fatigue soldiers based on where they can be treated.

(3) Duty cases (previously called mild) are those who are seen by a physician or physician assistant but who can be treated immediately and returned to duty in their small unit.

(4) Rest cases (previously called moderate) must be sent to their unit's nonmedical CSS elements for brief rest and light duties; rest cases do not require continual medical observation.

NOTE: Duty and rest cases are not medical casualties because they are still available for some duty in their units. However, those heavy cases who cannot return to duty or rest in their unit the same day are battle fatigue casualties.

(5) Hold cases are those who can be held for treatment at the triager's own medical treatment facility because both the tactical situation and the battle fatigue casualties' symptoms permit. This should be done whenever feasible.

(6) Refer cases are those who must be referred (and transported)

to a more secure or better-equipped medical treatment facility, either because of the tactical situation or the battle fatigue casualties' symptoms. Refer becomes hold when the soldiers reach a medical treatment facility where they can be held and treated.

NOTE: The hold and refer sublabels of heavy battle fatigue do not necessarily mean that a soldier is less likely to recover or will take longer to recover than cases treated as rest. However, the simple fact of holding or evacuation itself often prolongs the treatment and decreases likelihood of full recovery and return to duty.

    f.   There is no easy rule for deciding whether any specific symptom of battle fatigue makes the soldier a case of duty, rest, hold, or refer battle fatigue. That will require judgment based on—
    • What is known about the individual soldier.
    • The stressors involved.
    • How the soldier responds to helping actions.
    • What is likely to happen to the unit next.
    • What resources are available.

Battle fatigue symptoms can change rapidly based on a soldier's expectations. A successful combat stress control program prevents unnecessary evacuation and shifts battle fatigue cases from refer to the hold combat neuropsychiatric triage category. More importantly, it shifts many soldiers from hold category to rest and duty category. This allows them to recover in their units and keeps them from overloading the health service support system.

5-5. SEVERITY OF SYMPTOMS AND RESPONSE TO TREATMENT

    a.   The severity of symptoms and the speed and extent to which they respond to treatment are directly related to the intensity, lethality, and duration of the battle incidents which caused them. The following are general planning estimates which may be modified greatly by specific factors, such as unit cohesion, training, and leadership.

    b.   Leader and medical personnel in forward areas should expect as many or more soldiers to present with duty or rest battle fatigue as there will be hold and refer cases. It is essential that the former not become casualties by unnecessarily evacuating or holding them for treatment.

    c.   In general, the more intense the combat, especially with indirect fire and mass destruction, the more cases become heavy and need holding or referral, and the harder it is for them to recover quickly and return to duty.

    d.   Fifty to eighty-five percent of battle fatigue casualties (hold and refer) returned to duty following 1 to 3 days of restoration treatment, provided they are kept in the vicinity of their units (for example, within the division).

NOTE: When returned to their original units after successful treatment for battle fatigue, soldiers have no increased risk of relapse compared to their buddies who have not yet had battle fatigue. New soldiers who suffer battle fatigue during their first combat exposure deserve a second chance under supportive circumstances. They are no more likely to breakdown again than is another new replacement. However, it must be noted that treatment for battle fatigue will not turn a previously poor soldier into a good soldier. Soldiers who have accumulated too many terrible experiences may also reach a stage where reassignment to less dangerous duties is advised.

The variation of success rates between 50 and 85 percent can be due to several factors besides the intensity of the combat. Combat stress control planners must evaluate them critically. An 85 percent restoration rate could be the result of effective far forward treatment of true hold cases. Alternatively, it could occur because many easily treated cases are being held and rested in medical cots (and classified as hold) instead of being released to their units as duty or rest battle fatigue. That situation, in turn, could be due either to inadequate training and consultation to forward units or to a tactical situation which prevents maneuver units from resting any marginally effective soldiers.

    e.   Fifteen to fifty percent of battle fatigue casualties do not recover within 72 hours. The wide variation is due both to the intensity and nature of the battle and to the availability of far forward treatment. A large number of these battle fatigue casualties (10 to 40 percent of the original total) do return to some duty within 1 to 2 weeks. This is accomplished only if they continue structured, equally positive treatment. This treatment may be provided in a nonhospital-like atmosphere of a medical treatment (tactical) facility in the combat zone. Premature evacuation of battle fatigue soldiers out of the combat zone must be prevented as it often results in permanent psychiatric disability. If the tactical situation permits, the evacuation policy in the corps should be extended from 7 to 14 days for the reconditioning program, as this will substantially improve the returned to duty rate and decrease subsequent chronic disability.

f.   Five to fifteen percent of battle fatigue casualties fail to improve sufficiently to return to duty in the combat zone. Further reconditioning treatment can return many of these to useful duty in the COMMZ. Final evacuation to CONUS should not exceed 5 percent of total battle fatigue casualties. In retrospect, many of these soldiers have preexisting personalty types or other neuropsychiatric conditions which did not make them become battle fatigue casualties in the first place but did interfere with full recovery. A lesson plan on how to identify, treat, and prevent battle fatigue is provided in Appendix E.

CHAPTER 6

POST-TRAUMATIC STRESS DISORDER

6-1. INTRODUCTION

a. Over the years, there were sporadic reports of veterans from WWI, WWII, and the Korean conflict who suffered from persistent war neurosis or exhibited disturbed conduct. It was not until the late 1970s that PTSD was recognized as a classifiable psychiatric syndrome. A major driving force was the large number of Vietnam veterans who were suffering from what was at first labeled post-Vietnam syndrome (a pattern of symptoms). This syndrome involved varying combinations of anxiety and hyperarousal, depression and guilt, impulsive or violent behavior, social alienation or isolation, and often substance abuse. The common theme was the intrusive, painful memories of Vietnam and the ways the sufferer used to try to avoid or escape them. The post-Vietnam syndrome was also identified in noncombat military personnel. Similar symptoms and behavior were recognized in combat medics, hospital personnel and female nurses from Vietnam (and prior wars), and in ex-prisoners of war and concentration camp survivors.

b. Also in the mid-1970s, a similar syndrome was being recognized in some traumatic civilian situations, such as victims of natural or human-caused disasters, rape and other violent crimes, and terrorist acts or hostage-taking episodes. The same symptoms were found in many cases of burnout in civilian police, fire, and emergency medical personnel.

c. The American Psychiatric Association: *Diagnostic and Statistical Manual of Mental Disorders*, Third Edition, 1979, established the criteria for making a diagnosis of PTSD. These were updated in *Diagnostic and Statistical Manual of Mental Disorders*, Third Edition, Revised (DSM III-R), Washington, DC: American Psychiatric Association, 1987. See the DSM III-R's Diagnostic Criteria for PTSD for specifics.

d. The DSM III-R classification recognizes that PTSD can be—

• Acute (beginning within 6 months of the traumatic event, but not lasting longer than 6 months).

• Chronic (beginning within 6 months and lasting longer).

• Delayed (beginning or recurring after 6 months and perhaps even many years later).

Delayed PTSD can usually be related to other stressors going on in the person's life at the time, especially those which remind him of the combat stressors, such as a threat of loss of life, self-esteem, or love relationships.

e. It should be obvious when comparing the criteria with the description of battle fatigue in Chapter 5 that if a war or operations other than war continues for more than a month, some of the battle fatigue cases could meet the criteria for a diagnosis of PTSD. However, by US Army convention, the label PTSD will not be used while the soldier is in the theater of operations as battle fatigue more clearly implies the positive expectation of recovery and return to duty without persistent problems. The diagnosis of PTSD will be reserved for symptoms which persist or arise after the cessation of hostilities or after returning to the US.

6-2. PSYCHOLOGICALLY TRAUMATIC EVENTS

a. *Explanation of Psychological Trauma.* Psychological trauma, by definition, involves a crisis situation which makes the person feel he is changed for the worse. The implication is that the victim has suffered psychological injury and bears the psychological scars. To qualify under DSM III-R, the traumatic event must be something which is outside the range of usual human experience; it is an event which anyone would find horribly distressing. It is true that for professions like police, fire fighters, emergency medicine personnel, and the combat soldier many events come to be accepted as routine and even positive that other people would find unusual and traumatic. There remain, always, those terrible events (because of chance or mistake) that one hopes (and deep down believes) will never happen to oneself or one's close friends.

b. *Causes Contributing to Post-Traumatic Stress Disorder.* Traumatic events tend to be discrete events which provoke especially vivid memories of terror, horror, helplessness, failure, disgust, or "wrongness." Even in prolonged stress situations like being a PW or hostage or serving a medical or mortuary tour in Vietnam, subsequent PTSD will call out specific bad events. The events often (but not always) involve especially vivid sensory stimuli which are distinctly recorded in memory—visual images, smells, sounds, or feelings. The sense of "wrongness" may be from a personal violation or error, or from a sudden realization of the arbitrary unfairness in life as it affects others. So, for fire fighters, the death of children in fires is especially distressing. Combat soldiers who have killed enemies at long range in open battle with pride may be haunted years later by the memory of a soldier they killed in ambush. They are haunted because they searched the body for documents and instead found letters and photographs of loved ones similar to their own. Mortuary affairs personnel, too, tend to suffer when they inadvertently learn too much about the lives of the people whose bodies they must handle.

c. *Situations Likely to Provoke Post-Traumatic Stress Disorder.* The following is a listing of some of the situations in combat (and civilian equivalents):

- Loss of friends, buddies, and loved ones—
    - Under especially horrible circumstances.
    - With associated guilt because of an actual or perceived mistake or an error (omission or commission).
    - By having exchanged places so that a friend went and died instead of oneself.
- Injury or death to innocents (especially women and children).
- Seeing grossly mutilated bodies or wounds.
- Atrocities (done, condoned, or just observed).

• Lack of respect; lack of ceremony and "closure" for deceased friends.

• Lack of apparent meaning or purpose to the sacrifice, as might result from careless accidents or military errors.

• Inadequate quality of the homecoming reception which fails to validate the sacrifices and inhibits talking out the bad memories with family, friends, or fellow veterans.

    d.   *Symptoms of Post-Traumatic Stress Disorder.*

    (1) As the DSM III-R criteria reveal, PTSD is driven by intrusive memories of the traumatic event. These may come while awake or in dreams. The memories may come when a person is intoxicated. Occasionally these memories can be so vivid and multisensory that the person feels briefly he is reliving the experience (called a flashback). These thoughts are often triggered by sensory stimuli like those of the original events, such as objects, helicopter sounds, or smells. They become more intrusive for a while after the initial reminder. Because the memories are painful, the person with PTSD tries to avoid things that bring them on and may be quite successful.

    (2) The memories themselves do not constitute PTSD. The issue is whether (and how) they interfere with general well-being, happiness, and occupational or social functioning. For example, an infantry battalion colonel who had been a company commander in Vietnam described how he could still not see a piece of trash on the ground without suddenly becoming alert and being inclined to stay well away from it. Along with this would be painful, vivid memories of the horrible wounds which his young soldiers had suffered from booby-trapped trash. The colonel, however, does not see himself as scarred by those memories. Rather, he reassures himself that it was a hard lesson he has not forgotten and that if his unit should find itself in a similar war, he will see that his men do not have to learn this lesson in such a hard way again. He has reframed the painful memories in his mind so that they resulted in positive growth rather than an unhealed scar.

    (3) The colonel (mentioned above) did say that for several years after returning from Vietnam, he had experienced other symptoms which approached those of PTSD. He felt isolated and alienated

from other people, especially from civilians and other Army coworkers who had not been in Vietnam. He felt they could not understand what it was like and did not want to hear about it. He felt considerable anger towards them and held his temper chiefly by keeping to himself. He also tended to shut out his wife and children that way for a while.

(4) In more extreme cases, the isolation takes the form of an inability to feel affection or form close relationships. In losing close friends in combat, the soldier learned not to get too close again to the new replacements. The pattern has continued involuntarily. Negative feelings towards women and children (such as mistrust combined, perhaps, with guilt) may also have been acquired by the types of interactions encountered in the combat zone. The veterans with PTSD may go emotionally numb, continuing to function without any feeling when something happy or sad occurs.

(5) The angry and hostile feelings may stay tightly suppressed, as in the infantry colonel's experience described above, or they may erupt in angry outbursts or even in rage and violence. The ex-combat soldier who was once authorized to use lethal force in combat missions (and perhaps went beyond that to exercising force in the form of misconduct stress behaviors) has the memory of that power to provide temptation or self-justification for using violence again. This is especially likely when inhibition is impaired by alcohol or other intoxicant drugs. See Chapter 4 for details on misconduct stress behaviors.

(6) Substance abuse, especially alcohol, is common with PTSD. It provides an escape from or dulling of the memories. It is often used to try to get to sleep without the bad dreams and to reduce the anxiety and tension.

(7) Post-traumatic stress disorder characteristically involves symptoms of anxiety and hyperarousal—exaggerated startle responses or excessive alertness and vigilance for potential threats. These may be the threats of the past combat situation (such as the colonel's alertness about the trash or automatically noting potential ambush sites), or it may lead to excessive suspicion and caution in daily life (such as sleeping with a loaded pistol under the pillow or never sitting with one's back to a crowded room).

(8) Depressive symptoms, with poor sleep, loss of appetite and other pleasures, poor concentration, and guilt feelings are also characteristic of true PTSD. The sufferer is preoccupied with what he did or did not do to survive when others died. He may blame himself for mistakes that were real or quite beyond his control. He may have guilty thoughts, such as "If only I had not been so slow" or "If only I had been six feet closer, I would have seen that sniper before he shot my friend." The risk of suicide in PTSD is related to this depression and should not go unrecognized. It may also lead to reckless, potentially self-destructive behavior without conscious suicidal intent.

e.   *Early (Preventive) Treatment of Psychological Trauma.*

(1) An analogy has been made between psychic trauma and physical trauma, such as lacerated muscles and broken bones. People sometimes try to reassure the traumatized victim with the saying, "Time heals all wounds." This reflects the common observation that feelings of grief, loss, and guilt do normally tend to fade with time. But the analogy with physical wounds suggests the fallacy in such reassurance.

(2) Time heals broken bones, but only if they have been carefully realigned and stabilized to permit correct healing to begin. Time heals lacerated muscles, but only if they do not become badly infected by bacteria and dead tissue trapped in the wound. One of the most important lessons of combat wound surgery is not to attempt immediate primary closure (stitching the muscle and skin together again) as would be done in civilian hospital surgery. Instead, it is better to leave the wound open, keep it clean, and let it heal from the inside out for a few days. It can then be closed under sterile hospital conditions to decrease the size of the scar.

(3) With especially traumatic physical injuries, such as high-velocity bullet wounds, the surgical treatment is even more stringent. The surgeon provides immediate intervention to stop the bleeding. He then debrides dead tissue and surgically repairs the wound. In many cases the surgeon may delay primary closure and insert a drain which allows the wound to heal from the inside out.

(4) This analogy between physical traumatic injury and psychic traumatic stress appears accurate regarding immediate treatment. It

is best not to attempt immediate primary closure of psychic trauma by forcing the feelings out of mind and pressing on with other tasks that keep the disturbing feelings from surfacing. Instead, it is better to open up the psychic wound and let it drain. It may even be necessary to "insert a drainage tube" (to permit proper healing)—that is until the sufferer actually feels and expresses the suppressed, painful emotions and allows them to come out. This should be done as soon as the soldier who is suffering can pull back from the mission safely and regain (through brief rest and physical replenishment) the strength and clarity of mind needed to participate in his therapy.

(5) Another analogy perhaps more familiar to the nonmedical leader is the preventive maintenance of complex equipment. A good officer or NCO would not accept bringing an M1A1 tank (or an M16 rifle) back from fighting in a sandy desert or muddy/salt marsh without performing maintenance. This maintenance includes cleaning, re-oiling, and preparing the M1A1 tank for its next mission. The good leader knows that even though the dirt has not already jammed the weapon, the salt particles or sand grains will greatly increase corrosion and wear. The result could be unreliable performance, increased maintenance costs, later catastrophic failure, or maybe just a decreased useful life. Especially traumatic memories can have the same corrosive effect on the individual. They can impair the soldier's future performance. They can result in much unnecessary pain and suffering, both to the soldier and his family.

f.   *Small Group After-Action Debriefing.*

(1) Every small unit leader should routinely conduct after-action debriefings following any difficult situation. This is especially important if mistakes or misunderstandings occurred or losses were suffered. After-action debriefing for stress control may be integrated into the routine after-action review if the time available does not permit the separation of the two.

(2) The after-action review should be practiced in training and continued in conflict or war. The after-action review should be conducted as soon as it is safe for the leader to bring his team together. The purpose of the after-action review is to talk about the details of the recent action and agree on lessons learned. The first step

is to agree on what actually happened. It may be necessary to share everyone's observations to get a clear picture. The after-action review focuses on how well the battle/crew drill or TSOP worked. What went well and needs no change? What could use further improvement? What did not work at all and needs a new approach? When properly conducted, the after-action review increases understanding, trust, and cohesion within the team. It builds confidence that future events be handled even better.

(3) The after-action debriefing process shares the after-action review's concerns with details of what happened. It goes further by actively encouraging the team members to share and talk out their emotional responses to the event. After-action debriefings should also be routine during training, operations other than war, and war following any difficult or unpleasant event. Doing after-action debriefing routinely will make them second nature following any especially traumatic event. The objective of after-action debriefings following traumatic incidents is to promote "healing" by opening up, "cleaning and draining" any unpleasant or painful memories. Table 6-1 lists the key steps of the after-action debriefing process and Appendix A provides additional information.

(4) Leaders and buddies have the responsibility of continuing to talk through especially traumatic events. This should be done in a supportive way to individuals who show signs of distress in the after-action debriefings through personal conversations. Unit ministry teams may be helpful in the debriefings and in individual pastoral counseling to help the soldier redirect the painful memories toward positive spiritual growth. Individual referral to mental health/combat stress control personnel is indicated for severe distress.

TABLE 6-1. Key Steps in an After-Action Debriefing

- Explain the purpose and ground rules to be used during the debriefing at the outset.
- Involve everyone in verbally reconstructing the event in precise detail.
- Achieve a group consensus, resolving individual misperceptions and

misunderstandings and restoring perspective about true responsibility.

- Encourage expression (ventilation) of thoughts and feelings about the event.
- Validate feelings about the event as normal and work towards how they can be accepted, lived with, atoned.
- Prevent scapegoating and verbal abuse.
- Talk about the normal (but unpleasant) stress symptoms unit members experience and which may recur for a while, so they, too, can be accepted without surprise or fear of permanence.
- Summarize the lessons learned and any positive aspects of the experience.

---

g.   *Following Up the After-Action Debriefing.*

(1) People who live through extremely traumatic experiences should not expect to forget them. It is entirely normal to remember such events with sadness, resentment, guilt, or whatever emotions the event deserved. It may be appropriate to atone for mistakes made. It is also normal to dream about the event, even many years later. The "normal" pattern is for these painful feelings to become less intense and less frequent as they are balanced by later, positive events.

(2) Combat stress control/mental health personnel should always be notified whenever serious psychological trauma has occurred in a unit. They can assist command in assuring that the after-action debriefing process is done correctly. When indicated, the unit should arrange for combat stress control/mental health personnel to conduct a critical event debriefing. Critical event debriefings are similar to after-action debriefings but differ in the following ways:

• The critical event debriefing is led by a trained debriefer who is not a member of the unit being debriefed; the after-action debriefing is led by the small unit's own leader.

• The critical event debriefer explicitly defers issues of operational lessons learned in order to focus on the stress aspects and stress responses; the after-action debriefer does seek to capture relevant operational lessons learned in positive terms.

(3) Prior to redeployment home, units should schedule time

for everyone to verbally review the high and low points, talk through any unresolved issues, and conduct memorial ceremonies, if appropriate. Chaplains and combat stress control/mental health personnel should also take an important supportive role in these activities.

h. *Cautions for Preventive Intervention After Traumatic Stress.*

(1) The analogy between PTSD preventive interventions and traumatic wound surgery suggests a cautionary warning. If the surgery is not done skillfully, it can cause more harm than good, leaving dead tissue and bacteria in the wound. It may cut away tissue that did not need to be sacrificed, or realign the broken bones incorrectly. The same is potentially true for poorly executed after-action debriefings or critical event debriefings.

★　★　★

CAUTION

A poorly executed stress debriefing can cause harm. It can—
- **Leave important and painful issues unexplored, waiting to fester into future PTSD which will be harder to treat.**
- **Compound rather than relieve the feelings of guilt, anger, and alienation.**
- **Glamorize and encourage chronic PTSD disability.**

★　★　★

(2) The problem for early prevention efforts is to forewarn of possible post-traumatic stress symptoms without glamorizing them or advertising them as a reimbursable long-term disability. To do the latter invites malingering. It also subtly encourages those who do have real but not disabling post-traumatic symptoms to magnify them. This will be especially likely if they have other psychological issues or grievances which the symptoms also address, such as feeling unappreciated for the sacrifices suffered or guilt at having left their buddies.

(3) As with the treatment of acute battle fatigue, it is essential that all persons involved in preventive or treatment interventions for

PTSD express positive expectation of normal recovery. At the same time, they must indicate that continuing or recurring symptoms can and should be treated, still with positive expectation of rapid improvement. They should advise that post-traumatic stress symptoms may recur in the future at times of new stress. Successful treatment after future episodes should deal with the ongoing, new stressors as much as with the past trauma.

6-3. IDENTIFICATION AND TREATMENT OF POST-TRAUMATIC STRESS DISORDER AFTER THE WAR

a.   Because PTSD can recur months or years later (usually at times of added stress), coworkers and supervisors, chaplains, and health care providers should all be alert to the often subtle signs of PTSD long after combat. They should provide normalizing support and encourage (or refer the soldier for) mental health treatment.

b.   Remember, one of the common symptoms of PTSD is social alienation, withdrawal, and attempts to avoid reminders of the memories. Sufferers of post-traumatic stress symptoms are, therefore, not likely to volunteer their combat history or to admit easily to the "weakness" of not being able to control their painful memories. In fact, many soldiers with PTSD from prior combat (or accident or disaster) present as cases of substance abuse, family violence, or other misconduct. They will not receive the mental health help they deserve unless the causal stress relationship is explicitly asked about and recognized.

c.   Another hidden cost of inadequately treated post-traumatic stress will be the potentially large number of combat-experienced veterans (especially in the elite units) who either ask for transfer out of the combat unit, do not reenlist, or submit resignations. They will often say "My spouse wants me to leave the Army, and was especially worried that I almost got killed in that last deployment." Only with careful exploration will it become clear that the spouse is not upset with the Army or its risks but because the soldier came home changed. He keeps to himself, will not say what is wrong, gets mad at the children, drinks too much, and wakes up at night shouting and crying. The spouse thinks that if the soldier can only get away from the Army, he will get back to the way he was before. Unfortunately, if simply allowed to resign, whatever guilt, shame, or other traumatic memory is haunting him will probably continue unresolved.

6-4. COMBAT STRESS CONTROL (MENTAL HEALTH) PERSONNEL RESPONSIBILITIES

a. Combat stress control personnel have critical roles in assisting command in the prevention and early recognition of PTSD and in treatment of the individuals to avoid long-term suffering or disability following traumatic combat experiences. Treatment is often best when conducted in groups. The Department of Veterans Affairs (veterans' counseling centers) also may provide valuable consultation and treatment expertise. Whenever the Department of Veterans Affairs is involved, however, special care should be taken to avoid the negative expectation of long-term treatment and chronic disability reimbursement.

b. Post-traumatic stress disorder also occurs following natural and accidental disasters, terrorist attacks, rape or criminal assault, and hostage situations. Mental health/combat stress control teams have consistently demonstrated their value in rapid deployment of medical response teams for such contingencies. Their involvement following such incidents, as well as following combat, should be requested by the chain of command according to standing operating procedure.

CHAPTER 7

STRESS ISSUES
IN ARMY OPERATIONS

7-1. INTRODUCTION

This chapter reviews Army operational concepts for how we will fight. It highlights specific stressors that can contribute to decreased effectiveness, battle fatigue casualties, or misconduct stress behaviors. The chapter summarizes a number of other doctrinal manuals. For those readers who are already familiar with those manuals, it will highlight stress issues which were not explicitly stated in the original sources. For those readers who are not familiar with the source manuals, this chapter provides a hasty "one-stop" reference source. However, they are strongly encouraged to continue their education in the original references. All leaders must understand these operational realities and the words used to describe them. Leaders at all levels work closely with each other so they may be able to anticipate the stressors and prevent stress casualties.

7-2. OVERVIEW OF THE CHALLENGES

a. *Army Missions.* Army forces must meet worldwide strategic challenges against the full range of threats within highly varied operational theaters. In areas of greatest strategic concern, the Army must be prepared to fight battles of unprecedented scope and intensity. The operations surrounding such battles will routinely involve cooperation with other services and allies. While the threat of tactical nuclear war has decreased, it may be present in some confrontations. The threat of functioning on a chemical or biological battlefield remains a possibly in any conflict, anywhere in the world.

NOTE: Every scenario involves its own unique combination of stressors which must be controlled to assure that our forces function at their best.

b. *Joint and Combined Operations.* The nature of modern battle and the broad dispersion of US geographical interests require joint operations by US forces. It is imperative that Army units fight as part of a joint team with units of the US Air Force, the US Navy, and the US Marine Corps. We must cooperate with representatives of civilian and government agencies. These agencies may include the State Department, Central Intelligence Agency, Federal Bureau of Investigation, Red Cross, United Nations, and international relief agencies. It is also critical that commanders prepare themselves and their troops to fight in coalition/combined warfare alongside the forces of our nation's allies. Teamwork in joint and combined operations will be necessary in any battle the Army forces fight, as well as in operations other than war.

(1) Leaders must take active steps to counteract prejudices, disrespect, mistrust, and doubt about the reliability and competence of other services and allies. It is extremely important that soldiers respect those beliefs that are different from our own and respect the customs and practices of people in other nations. Unchecked prejudices, disrespect, mistrust, and doubt can lead to high battle fatigue casualties or to misconduct stress behaviors which could damage the coalition.

(2) When directed by the national command authority (NCA), the Army may need to assist a less-developed host nation (HN) in setting up an effective stress control or community mental health/social services system. This system may be for its Armed Forces, refugees, and/or civilian population.

c. *Forward Presence Versus Contingency Operations.* Army operations in the foreseeable future will be fought in one of two basic environments.

(1) One environment may be an anticipated theater of war

with an existing support structure of communications, air defense, logistic facilities, and ports. Service families may be present in the theater before the conflict. Their presence adds additional concern for their security and for noncombatant evacuation operations. The troops and their families must have confidence that the chain of command can be trusted to implement a workable plan to assure the safety of the families. Otherwise, the soldiers' first concern will be the safety of their family rather than mission accomplishment.

(2) The other environment may be a relatively austere theater. In this environment, Army leaders will have to choose between creating such a support base or fighting with only external support. Contingency operations are military actions requiring rapid deployment in response to a crisis. Contingency operations involving Army forces may provide a rapid show of force in support of a threatened ally to deter aggression by a hostile neighbor. Contingency operations react to the invasion of a friendly government, protect lives and property of US nationals, rescue hostages, or perform other tasks as directed by the NCA. The size of a contingency force, its mission, and its area of operations will vary.

(a) Rapid deployment itself involves much physical and mental stress during preparation and transportation. If the deployment crosses many time zones, there is the added disruption of the body's biological day-night/work-rest cycles.

(b) The necessity for secrecy in contingency operations puts great stress on the soldiers who are suddenly "sealed in." Great stress is also placed on their families with whom they cannot communicate. Leadership must ensure and support the establishment of family support groups. They must also be sensitive to the needs of families to learn about the involvement of their spouses in particular military operations. Stress control leader actions are discussed in Appendix A.

d. *Austere Support.* Army forces must be prepared to fight their battles at the end of long, vulnerable lines of logistical support, with limited availability of airlift and sealift. They must anticipate high consumption rates for all supplies. They may have to fight outnumbered against an enemy with significantly shorter supply lines. This may be true for leading US echelons even in a contingency operation against a distant opponent much smaller than the United States. Logistical support may be austere in such situations and thereby markedly affect the design of campaigns and the planning and conduct of battles.

NOTE: Shortages and uncertainties of resupply contribute to low morale and high rates of battle fatigue casualties unless troops are psychologically prepared to improvise. Once apprised of the situation, they must believe that everything feasible is being done to support them.

    e.   *Urban Combat.* Combat in built-up areas will be unavoidable in war and operations other than war (conflict). Units will have to plan for attack and defense in urban areas and for fluid battles around them. The usual static, house-to-house nature of urban warfare, with many snipers, mines, and booby traps, tends to increase battle fatigue casualties unless troops are well-trained and led. Built-up areas are also likely to provide temptations for looting, alcohol and substance abuse, black marketeering, and harmful social interactions. Preventive measures must be in place to avoid these temptations. For more detailed information, refer to FMs 90-10 and 90-10-1.

    f.   *Presence of Civilians and Rules of Engagement.* The likely presence of civilians in combat areas can have diverse effects. Seeing and perhaps accidentally inflicting casualties on civilians (especially if they are women and children) increases battle fatigue, especially if the civilians are perceived as friendly. If the civilians are hostile, or have been infiltrated by enemy partisans, the potential for misconduct stress behaviors is high unless strong unit cohesion and a sense of ethical purpose protects against it.

    g.   *Continuous Operations.* Continuous land combat is an advanced warfare concept made possible by the almost complete mechanization of land combat forces. It is also made possible by the technology that permits effective movement and target detection at night, in poor weather, and in other low-visibility conditions. Combat can continue around the clock at the same high level of intensity for extended periods. Armies now have the potential to fight without letup. The reasons that have traditionally forced a pause—darkness, resupply, regrouping—have been largely overcome by technological advances. Thus, CONOPS is more possible due to advanced technology, and the demands of such operations are very stressful. However, the possibility of failure of the sophisticated devices can also be a great stressor. Soldiers who become dependent on the technology in their military occupational specialty could feel extremely vulnerable should the equipment fail. Where possible, soldiers should be taught how to accomplish the task without the device so that its failure would not be so catastrophic. Refer to FM 25-101 for doctrine on battle-focused training. For recommendations related to CONOPS leader actions, see FM 22-9 and Appendix A of this FM.

h. *Sustained Operations.* The term *sustained operations* (SU-SOPS) is used when the same soldiers and small units engage in CONOPS with no opportunity for the unit to stand down. This permits very little opportunity for soldiers to catch more than a few minutes of sleep under disruptive conditions. Weapons systems can operate day and night, but must be refueled, rearmed, and repaired by soldiers for their operations. Soldiers need water, food, hygiene, and sleep just as the machines need refueling and preventive maintenance. Sustained operations should be avoided whenever possible except for brief periods, when forced by enemy action or accepted by command as essential to maintain pressure on a disintegrating enemy or catch him at a disadvantage. Sustained operations must always be considered carefully as a calculated risk. Leader actions when SUSOPS must be undertaken are discussed in Appendix A.

NOTE: Sustained operations place significant emphasis on the leaders' abilities to implement effective sleep plans (which include the leaders) and on cross-training of soldiers so they can perform a variety of roles during combat operations. Continuous operations do not necessarily involve SUSOPS if sufficient units (or individuals within units) are available to allow everyone to get adequate rest. Leaders must be aware that SUSOPS quickly deplete the combat effectiveness of units physically, logistically, and psychologically. For CONOPS, plans must be in place to relieve spent units and redesignate missions to other less depleted organizations.

7-3. THE POTENTIAL BATTLEFIELD

a.   The threat will vary according to the intensity and location of the conflict. A European, Southwest Asian, and possibly Northwest Asian scenario would most likely be a high-intensity environment. This environment would be characterized by broad frontages, deep targets, and enemy penetrations of varying depths. Operations other than war (conflicts) are usually associated with Third World countries. These conflicts would be characterized by poorly defined frontages, semiautonomous dismounted operations conducted at varying depths, and rear area security problems.

b.   Each environment would challenge (stress) friendly logictics—including medical—in terms of distances and amounts required. Each environment would also provide opportunities for deep strikes, long-range unconventional operations, and terrorism. Prepared airfields, permanent bases, and fixed support facilities (including medical units and facilities) will become primary targets for opposing forces. In the wartime environment, such facilities may not survive. In the operations other than war environment, logistical and command centers may have to be highly centralized for defense, thus lengthening already long lines of communications.

7-4. ARMY OPERATIONS DOCTRINE: IMPLICATIONS FOR COMBAT STRESS

a.   Basics of Army Operations.

(1) Army operations described in FM 100-5 (the Army's keystone doctrinal manual) emphasize battlefield success through five basic tenets—initiative, depth, agility, synchronization, and versatility. These tenets apply to everyone and every unit in the Army. Table 7-1 identifies each tenet, the stress issue associated with that tenet, and recommended actions for commanders and leaders.

(2) The most violent and high-risk environment is that of war with its associated combat operations.

b.   *Opposing Forces on the Battlefield.* The opposing forces on the modern battlefield will rarely fight across orderly, distinct lines. Massive concentrations of forces and fires will make penetrations all but inevitable and will result in a nonlinear battlefield. There may be little distinction between rear and forward areas.

c. *Reliance on Traditional American Military Qualities.* Army operations doctrine utilizes the traditional military qualities of skill, tenacity, boldness, and courage, together with the technological prowess, self-reliance, and aggressive spirit which characterizes the American soldier. While respecting the increased complexity and lethality of modern weapons, Army doctrine recognizes that such weapons are no better than the soldier's skill and mastery he brings to bear on the enemy.

7-5. ENDURANCE/STAYING POWER ON THE BATTLEFIELD

In addition to initiative, agility, depth, synchronization, and versatility, Army operations will demand endurance. Endurance is the ability of a force to sustain high levels of combat potential relative to its opponent over the duration of a campaign. American soldiers have proven their staying power under adversity. This quality of endurance can make the difference between victory and defeat.

TABLE 7-1. Combat Stress Issues and the Battlefield Imperatives

INITIATIVE

STRESS ISSUES	RECOMMENDED ACTIONS FOR COMMANDERS AND LEADERS
Subordinates must accomplish commander's intent without direct orders.	Practice stating intent clearly and simply.
Requires corporal to colonel to be planners and problem solvers.	Teach problem solving and planning skills at all levels.
Taking action with little information.	Let junior leaders be responsible without overmanagement.
Taking action while improvising.	Develop leadership programs which reward improvisation.
Taking action without ideal force ratios, equipment, support, or communications.	Practice fighting with less and achieving more.
Deterioration in ability to see patterns and make decisions due to sleep loss and stress.	Practice sleep planning and stress control techniques.
	Train in smoke, MOPP, and adverse weather.

DEPTH

STRESS ISSUES	RECOMMENDED ACTIONS FOR COMMANDERS AND LEADERS
Planning well-ahead in both space and time.	Push intelligence information to lower levels.
Isolating own men and units, some for an extended time.	Train to fight with few resources and realistic battle losses.
Surviving in isolation, with uncertain resupply.	Learn to function in isolation. Teach ways to live and survive by self.
Risking high casualties.	Emphasize hope, and mission accomplishment despite the odds.
Some units seen as being expendable.	Train survival skills to all soldiers/units.

AGILITY

STRESS ISSUES	RECOMMENDED ACTIONS FOR COMMANDERS AND LEADERS
Thinking quickly, and making decisions.	Build soldier loyalty to support quick reaction to mission changes.
Moving fast and switching objectives.	Practice ways to ensure all soldiers are clear on mission changes and role responsibilities.
Reacting to sudden mission changes.	Practice how to plan and execute with short notice.
Communicating with subordinate and neighboring units.	Practice communications using multiple or redundant means.
Slowing in performance and mental ability due to sleep loss and stress.	Practice sleep discipline and measures to prevent fatigue.
	Train in smoke, MOPP, and adverse environment.

SYNCHRONIZATION

STRESS ISSUES	RECOMMENDED ACTIONS FOR COMMANDERS AND LEADERS
Unity of effort, even though dispersed. Massing rapidly, increasing the chances of casualties from friendly fire.	Build trust and confidence in other units, supporting arms and services.
Explicit coordination among units.	Overpractice communications (soldiers and units).
Participation in coordination of mission with less dependence on primary communications nets.	Collect and evaluate information from a variety of traditional and non-traditional sources.
Interpreting ways in which friendly and enemy capabilities interact.	Use interactive decision-making models.
Deterioration in communication skills due to sleep loss, stress, lack of hydration, and adverse environments.	Ensure sleep discipline, adequate water intake, and acclimatization for all personnel.

VERSATILITY

STRESS ISSUES	RECOMMENDED ACTIONS FOR COMMANDERS AND LEADERS
Completing an operation while shifting the focus toward the next operations.	Practice ways to ensure all soldiers are clear on mission changes and role responsibilities.
Splitting elements of the unit during tailoring of the task force.	Conduct task force training and develop unit cohesion while building trust and confidence in other units and elements.
Changing the combat mission of destroying to rebuilding.	Build soldier's loyalty to support quick reaction to mission changes and new objectives.
Suddenly changing from high arousal activity to forced inactivity (or vice versa).	Develop constructive ways of letting off steam and of gearing up and down.
Rapidly moving from one geograph-ical region to another and from one type of warfare to another in quick succession.	Practice soldier survival skills while training in adverse environments.

CHAPTER 8

STRESS AND STRESSORS ASSOCIATED WITH OFFENSIVE/DEFENSIVE OPERATIONS

8-1. INTRODUCTION

The effects of stress and stressors associated with offensive and defensive operations are immense. Leaders must understand how high levels of stress can affect the performance of their personnel in offensive and defensive operations.

8-2. OFFENSIVE OPERATIONS

a. *Fundamentals.* (See FM 100-5 for details.)

(1) The offensive is the decisive form of war—the commander's ultimate means of imposing his will upon the enemy. Even in the defense, seizing the initiative requires offensive operations. Combat service support units, by the nature of their missions, will usually be in tactical defense even while the units they support are on the attack. However, the likelihood of rear battle requires that all leaders fully understand the principles, tactics, and psychological advantages of going on the offense.

(2) Commanders, while shielding their own troops from stress, should attempt to promote terror and disintegration in the opposing force. Aggressive patrolling, raids, and sudden, violent actions (which catch the enemy by surprise and do not permit him to re-

cover) should be common tools to magnify the enemy's battlefield stress. Stress-creating actions can hasten the destruction of his combat capability. Some examples of stress-creating actions are attacks on his command structure; the use of artillery, air-delivered weapons, smoke; deception; psychological warfare; and the use of special operations forces. Such stress-creating actions can hasten the destruction of the enemy's capability for combat.

b. *Purposes.* While offensive operations may have as their objective the destruction or neutralization of an enemy force, inflicting physical damage is frequently incidental to offensive success. Large gains are achieved by destroying the coherence of the defense, fragmenting and isolating enemy units in the zone of the attack, and driving deep to secure operationally decisive objectives. These have the result of "stressing out" the enemy defenders.

c. *Characteristics.* The most successful offensive operations are characterized by surprise, concentration, speed, flexibility, and audacity.

d. *Phases.* The four general phases of offensive operations are preparation, attack, exploitation, and pursuit.

e. *Forms of Maneuver.* Just as similar phases are common to all offensive operations, similar forms of maneuver are common to all attacks. These forms of maneuver include envelopment, turning movement, infiltration, penetration, and frontal attack.

f. *Conducting Offensive Operations.* Offensive operations are characterized by aggressive initiative on the part of subordinate commanders, by rapid shifts in the main effort to take advantage of opportunities, by momentum, and by the deepest, most rapid destruction of enemy defenses possible.

g. *Offensive Framework.* A simple, complete concept of operation is the basis of all tactical offensive actions.

8-3. BATTLE FATIGUE AND BATTLE FATIGUE CASUALTIES IN THE OFFENSE

a. The preparation for an attack is a time of high stress and anxiety, both for novice soldiers and for veterans. Physical stress complaints (musculoskeletal, cardiorespiratory, gastrointestinal) are common at sick call. If morale is low and troops are pessimistic about the attack, battle fatigue casualties and misconduct stress behaviors may be high.

b.   There may be much stress and physical fatigue in the attack, exploitation, and pursuit phases; but relatively few battle fatigue casualties occur as long as soldiers are able to continue moving and advancing. Battle fatigue casualties increase if the advance bogs down, is pinned down, or loses momentum, especially when indirect fire is received. Being bombed or shelled in the starting line is notoriously disruptive, as is being hit by friendly fire (a risk inherent in a fluid fast-moving battle). Diversionary attacks or security operations may lack the strong psychological motivation of the main attack and require additional positive explanation by leaders to minimize adverse combat stress behaviors.

c.   Units in reserve have the difficult task of maintaining fighting spirit and readiness. While not yet fighting, they are at risk but must try to stay rested. The junior troops usually get some sleep if they are not too apprehensive. The leaders often do not get enough sleep because of the never-ending planning and briefing cycle. It is most important that leaders do plan for and get enough sleep themselves and maintain good hydration and nutrition.

d.   Combat support and CSS troops (especially supply, transport, maintenance, and medical) may be tasked for prolonged SUSOPS, with increased risk from enemy forces which were bypassed. They tend to have more battle fatigue casualties per WIA than the combat arms when they do take casualties. Seeing (and especially having to touch) the maimed bodies left behind by the attack may produce battle fatigue (and/or future PTSD) in inadequately prepared troops even if they are not themselves under fire.

e.   Every effort should be made to provide rest in the combat and field trains for exhausted soldiers. Restoration treatment for battle fatigue casualties should be at medical treatment facilities as close behind the attack as possible. This should generally be possible in the division support area and brigade support area.

f.   Misconduct stress behaviors which constitute criminal acts such as looting, killing EPW, rape, and other atrocities against noncombatants and "liberation" of alcohol and drugs are always a risk when victorious troops advance into enemy territory. Leaders must lead by example and retain control, discipline, and a sense of pride to preclude such behavior.

8-4. DEFENSIVE OPERATIONS

a.   *Fundamentals.* (See FM 100-5 for details.) Defensive operations retain ground, gain time, deny the enemy access to an area, damage or defeat attacking forces, and save one's own units.

b.   *Purposes.* The immediate purpose of any defense is to defeat the attack.

c.   *Characteristics.* In any defensive plan, preparation, disruption, concentration, and flexibility are fundamental.

d.   *Defensive Patterns.* While defensive operations may take many forms, traditional usage divides defensive arrangements into two broad categories: mobile and area defenses.

e.   *Defensive Framework.* A simple, complete concept of operations is the basis of all defenses. Defenses are organized into five complementary elements:

- Security force operations.
- Defensive operations.
- Reserve operations.
- Deep operations.
- Rear operations.

NOTE: Each of these five defensive elements entails different stress for the defending troops and may evoke different combat stress behaviors.

f.   *Retrograde Operations.* A retrograde operation is a movement to the rear or away from the enemy. Retrograde operations are executed to gain time, preserve forces, avoid combat under undesirable conditions, or draw the enemy into an unfavorable position.

8-5. STRESS, BATTLE FATIGUE, AND BATTLE FATIGUE CASUALTIES IN THE DEFENSE

a.   *Stressful Uncertainties.* Defensive operations involve more stressful uncertainty about enemy intentions and capabilities than being on the offensive. The defensive posture itself implies that the enemy has the greater strength. Rumors and appraisals of the situation are more likely to be pessimistic and may overmagnify the true threat.

b. *Mobile Defenders.* Mobile defense incurs more physical fatigue, but soldiers are less likely to become battle fatigue casualties. Even in such obviously high-risk situations, such as a covering force in contact with an overwhelmingly strong attacking enemy, a positive unit identity and cohesion can provide remarkable protection against fear. Problems with battle fatigue and misconduct stress behaviors are more likely to occur later in the survivors who make it back to a safe location—these may cause difficulties for reconstitution of the units.

c. *Static Defenders.* The stressors in static defense vary with the degree of comfort and security provided by the fortifications. If very strong, the fortifications may increase confidence to the point of complacency and degraded vigilance; if less strong and subjected to intense or prolonged bombardment, static defense incurs high battle fatigue casualty rates. Discomfort, especially cold, wet conditions with inability to move around, increases both cold injury and battle fatigue casualties.

d. *Hidden Stress Casualties (in Retrograde Operations).* There are relatively few diagnosed battle fatigue casualties in retrograde operations. There may be many undiagnosed battle fatigue soldiers. Some of these soldiers may be ineffective; others may be a loss to their unit as a result of becoming a PW, MIA, WIA, or KIA. Misconduct stress behaviors, such as alcohol abuse, desertion, or criminal acts (looting, rape, atrocities, and the murder of leaders), may occur if the retrograde operation becomes disorganized. The danger of retreat is that it may degenerate into mass panic or rout with every man (or small team) trying to save himself at the expense of the others. Such panic, spread by fleeing soldiers and fanned by rumor, is contagious. Unless checked quickly, it leads to the catastrophic failure of entire armies and the nation, as befell France under the German blitzkrieg of 1940.

CHAPTER 9

COMBAT STRESS CONTROL IN OPERATIONS OTHER THAN WAR

9-1. INTRODUCTION

The Army classifies its activities during peacetime and conflict as operations other than war. Conflict is characterized by hostilities short of war to secure strategic objectives.

a.   The growing incidence of conflict pits Army forces against irregular or unconventional forces, enemy special operations forces (SOF), and terrorists. Conflict poses a threat to US interests at all times, not just in periods of active hostilities. United States citizens, especially military personnel and their families, may be at risk anywhere in the world.

b.   The terrorist or guerrilla forces count on fear and terror as their principal weapon and objective. By attacking the defending military forces and civilian population only at times and places of their choosing, they deny the defender any safe areas and flaunt the inability of the authorities to protect themselves or their people. By hiding among the populace and using women and children as combatants, the guerrilla or terrorist provokes the defending forces to perceive the people as unworthy of protection. The defender may adopt harsh repressive measures and commit atrocities which turn the people against the defenders.

(1) Although the stressors of terrorism and guerrilla tactics are less overwhelming than those of war, they are deliberately designed to cause breakdown of military professionalism and discipline. As these events are reported in the media, the enemy expects that the home front in the US will perceive the conflict as unwinnable and

immoral. The goal for the enemy is for the US home front to abandon support for the effort and even turn against our own soldiers.

(2) In operations other than war when combat operations are required (engagements), battle fatigue casualty rates rarely exceed one battle fatigue casualty per ten WIA. Other misconduct stress behaviors, including drug and alcohol abuse and criminal acts, become the more common and serious reflectors of combat stress in light combat operations. Table 9-1, pages 121–122, lists some likely stress-producing aspects of operations other than war which involve conflict.

(3) Civil and military leaders would be in error to rely only on military technology and indiscriminate firepower to oppose a guerrilla force. These leaders must also recognize and defuse the political and psychological stress threat. If they fail to do this, they may win the battles in the field but still lose the war (or the post-treaty peace).

c. Forces for military operations other than war must be selected and task-organized to fit the situation. Combat, when it occurs, is strategically defensive and intended to permit political, social, and economic development activities. The nature of the conflict requires that coercive measures be the minimum necessary to achieve the purpose. This will be visible to the soldier largely in terms of extremely restrictive rules of engagement. For his own sake, as well as for the success of the mission, the soldier must understand the environment in which he is to operate and fight.

(1) Army actions in operations other than war must be fully coordinated with national strategy and fused at the operational level into a coherent effort. The effort must complement economical, political, and military activities. This linkage with such activities must be made clear to the soldiers. Failure to do so can lead to confusion and frustration among soldiers as to the purpose, attainability, and objectives of their mission.

(2) Public affairs plays a critical role in the operations other than war environment, across all of the operational categories. It supports the commander and soldier by—

> • Assessing information needs.
> • Formulating messages.
> • Facilitating the flow of information.

• Providing communications channels.

• Serving as the primary interface between the military and the civilian media.

A key public affairs mission is to reduce the soldiers' sense of isolation by—

• Reinforcing the role each soldier plays in the operation.

• Ensuring information flows in and out of the theater.

• Telling the Army story to the public in order to maintain support for the effort and the soldiers.

(3) Operations other than war (peacetime or conflict) require that the plan and the task organization of units be tailored to the specific operation. The following paragraphs review the operational categories and the special stressors that soldiers are likely to encounter.

TABLE 9-1. Stress-Producing Aspects of Operations Other Than War (Conflict)

- Operational purpose or mission often not clear—when and how forcefully to fight.
- Restriction on fire power and force ratio to prevent destroying the civilian countryside.
- Frustration over not finding the enemy.
- Likely to be physically grueling operations.
- Living off the land.
- Living and fighting in unfamiliar country.
- Police duties or combat in urban terrain.
- Living and fighting without typical support and "creature comforts."
- Contrast between support troops living in comparative luxury while combat soldiers live more austerely.
- Long periods of hard marching without making contact with enemy.
- Continuing conflict with slow progress.
- Taking, then abandoning, then retaking the same terrain, with casualties each time.
- Unsure of when, where, and how the attack is coming.
- Unable to decisively engage the enemy.

- Difficulty distinguishing the enemy from noncombatant local population.
- Frustration that locals are helping the enemy.
- Tendency to develop "bunker mentality" and lose vigilance.
- Lack of confidence in fighting on enemy soil.
- Waiting extended periods for enemy contact; boredom from lack of activities.
- Overreacting to the enemy's "hit-and-run" tactics.
- Rules of engagement may prohibit firing until fired on.
- Being ambassadors versus warriors.
- Developing a sense of superiority to local citizens of less developed countries.
- Low esteem for locals because many become prostitutes or sellers of black market goods.
- Availability of illegal drugs and alcohol creates temptation.

9-2. SUPPORT FOR INSURGENCY OPERATIONS

a. Support for insurgency is a goal-directed activity. These operations are normally of long duration and predominantly conducted by indigenous or surrogate forces. These forces are organized, trained, equipped, supported, and directed in varying degrees by an outside source. Unconventional warfare, a tactic employed in insurgency or counterinsurgency, includes guerrilla warfare and other direct offensive, low-visibility, covert, or clandestine operations. It also includes the indirect activities of subversion, sabotage, intelligence collection, evasion, and escape. The primary forces used in unconventional warfare are SOF. Combat stress control personnel who support such operations must have the appropriate level of security clearance to debrief and treat SOF personnel at the conclusion of their mission.

b. Insurgency is an organized, armed, political struggle whose goal may be the seizure of power through revolutionary takeover and the replacement of the existing government. In some cases, however, insurgency is undertaken to break away from government control and establish an autonomous state within traditional ethnic or religious territorial bounds. It may even be conducted to extract limited political concessions that are unattainable with less violent means.

(1) The existing government will attempt to isolate the insurgents from the general population. Therefore, insurgents normally must live under austere or primitive conditions, have limited or no

access to medical care, and often operate using hit-and-run tactics. The severity of those conditions will depend upon how much support the insurgents receive from the local population and the effectiveness of the government's repressive measures.

(2) If the US SOF were to provide support to a US-backed insurgent group, they would also operate and live in this austere environment. Issues which would contribute to combat stress, battle fatigue, and potential misconduct stress behaviors are listed in Table 9-2 along with leader and buddy actions to counteract these stressors.

TABLE 9-2. Stress Considerations and Recommendations for Stress Control in Insurgency Operations

STRESS ISSUES IN UNCONVENTIONAL WARFARE/SUPPORT TO INSURGENCY	RECOMMENDED LEADER/BUDDY ACTIONS
Isolation (lack of world news).	Build unit cohesiveness and strong sense of US SOF identity.
Secrecy about own activities.	Command emphasis on keeping field operatives informed and explaining reasons for policy changes (consistent with operations security).
Cultural differences and language barriers.	Special training for the local culture.
Austere and primitive living conditions.	Meaningful and military-related activities, such as training, improved living conditions, and such.
Hiding out; enforced inactivity with high tension. Observation of atrocities (by both forces). Overidentification with the insurgents, such as adoption of local customs at odds with US customs/rules/laws.	Unit after-action debriefings working through problems encountered or incidents witnessed.
Difficulty withdrawing (emotionally as well as logistically) when the mission or US policy changes.	Period of time within the unit after the operations for wind down and defusing.

(3) Insurgents frequently adopt terrorism as a tactic. This is one of the things that makes counterinsurgency so difficult. It also makes support for insurgency (should we be called upon to do it) such a moral dilemma.

(4) Insurgencies and use of terrorism independent of insurgencies probably pose stress which is as severe as that which occurs in the most violent of "conventional" wars. All the societal norms which Americans accept seem to be abandoned and perhaps irrelevant. The participants' moral compass may go haywire so that they have a hard time distinguishing right from wrong. Innocent persons are singled out for the most atrocious attacks because of their shock value.

(5) Inspired, compassionate leadership and firm discipline are required to prevent misconduct stress behaviors.

9-3. SUPPORT FOR COUNTERINSURGENCY OPERATIONS

Internal Defense and Development (IDAD) strategy is the full range of measures taken by a nation to promote its growth and protect itself from subversion, lawlessness, and insurgency. It focuses on building viable institutions (political, economic, military, and social) that respond to the needs of the society. Developmental programs, carefully planned, implemented, and publicized, can serve the interests of the population groups and deny exploitable issues to the insurgents. Foreign Internal Defense (FID) is the participation by civilian and military agencies of a government in any of the action programs taken by another government to free and protect its society. Foreign Internal Defense is the US role in the IDAD strategy.

a.   In countering an insurgency, the Army may employ specially trained forces or training teams. This sort of activity may include the transfer of defense equipment, the training of foreign soldiers, advisory assistance, or even the commitment of combat forces. All military efforts in a counterinsurgency campaign will be made in concert with the HN and the initiatives of other US government agencies involved to ensure a synchronized national effort.

b.   The forces selected for FID will depend on the threat to be countered. Special operations forces, light and heavy forces, aviation units, logistical support, and a variety of training teams may be used for counterinsurgency efforts.

    c.   The high degree of selection and training, provided it is done well, tends to minimize battle fatigue and misconduct stress behaviors. However, if units are hastily selected and deployed, they are likely to have problems facing the special stressors in operations other than war (listed in Table 9-1).

    d.   Refer to Table 9-3 for mental health considerations and recommendations in support of counterinsurgency operations.

9-4. COMBATTING TERRORISM

    a.   Terrorism and the threat of terrorism are widespread in the modern world. Terrorism can occur throughout the operational continuum. It is defined as the unlawful use or threatened use of force or violence against people or property to coerce or intimidate governments or societies, often to achieve political, religious, or ideological objectives.

    (1) Terrorists may be independent groups or may be supported covertly or openly by hostile states. Terrorist organizations sometimes cooperate with each other in pursuit of common strategic objectives.

    (2) US Army doctrine calls for preventive action (antiterrorism) along with reactive measures (counterterrorism) to meet the terrorist threat to US forces, representatives, and agencies and to the security of American citizens and property.

    (a) Antiterrorism consists of those defensive measures used to reduce the vulnerability of personnel, family members, facilities, and equipment to terrorist acts.

    (b) Counterterrorism is comprised of those offensive measures taken to prevent, deter, and respond to terrorism. Terrorism must be dealt with in the Army's daily operations as well as being of concern in war and operations other than war. Terrorist tactics may be directed at service families, recreational facilities, and general targets such as commercial airliners.

TABLE 9-3. Stress Considerations and Recommendations for Stress Control in Counterinsurgency Operations

SUPPORT FOR COUNTERINSURGENCY STRESSORS	RECOMMENDATIONS AND ACTIONS
Cultural conflicts. Language barriers. Climate differences. Unfamiliar terrain.	Develop an effective sponsorship program. Ensure acclimatization of troops and required training.
Difficulty identifying the enemy.	Establish HN education program with emphasis on understanding local culture, values, practices, and pressure affecting HN people.
Reaction to hit-and-run tactics.	Provide time for soldiers to debrief on their experience.
Support troops versus combat soldiers living standards.	Do not overbuild support base.
Soldier and family unclear concerning Army's mission.	Using a variety of media, continue to explain the unit's mission.
Continuing the fight with slow progress.	Educate soldiers on realities of the mission.
Dealing with extended periods of no activity.	Provide relevant training during lulls.
Inability to decisively engage opposition.	After completion of the operations, conduct debriefings. Discuss what occurred, individual reactions and feelings, and strengths and weaknesses of the operation. Link accomplishments with unit goals.
Host-nation support roles.	Leadership clearly communicates soldiers' roles, rules of engagement, and reason or rationale for rules to HN leadership's own forces.

(c) Awareness of the threat and recognition that the indicators of terrorist activity differ from those of the enemy on the conventional battlefield are essential to combatting terrorism.

(d) Leaders at all levels must develop a broad view of this threat which will guide them in securing their operations and in protecting their soldiers from terrorists as well as from conventional enemy military forces.

(e) At the same time, they must not impose excessive anxiety, restrictions, and repression which play into the enemies' game plan.

(3) United States counterterrorism forces must be protected against and treated for combined effects of frustration, moral conflict, and boredom which are the terrorists' main goals for success. When implementing preventive or reactive programs, the following should be considered:

• Battle fatigue is usually mild and can be managed in the units.

• Special programs may be needed to prevent and treat alcohol and drug misuse.

• Additional programs may be required to prevent misconduct against prisoners or noncombatants and other lapses of military discipline.

• Soldiers who return from counterterrorism missions and other special operations need a stand-down period. This should come before they are reunited with their families or other noncombatants. The stand-down period is needed to "defuse" the tension that has built up during the operational phase.

These programs are also needed to protect against PTSD which may disable the soldier or veteran for several months or years after returning home.

b. Terrorist acts produce debilitating stress reactions due to the shock of the event, the sudden violation of familiar and safe settings, and the feeling of loss of control. The stress may impact not only on the direct victims of the terrorist act but also on the passive witnesses of the destruction, the immediate rescuers and care givers, and the more distant care givers, friends, coworkers, and family. The following feelings or behaviors may become evident.

• Hostile feelings (repressed or expressed).

• Feelings of dependence.

• Feelings of powerlessness or incompetence.

• Regressive behaviors (childish temper outbursts, stubbornness).

• Negative responses to relocation and isolation.

• Positive identification with the terrorists ("the Stockholm syndrome").

• Sense of being a victim.

• Negative feelings about one's own country or its allies.

   c.   Victims of disaster/hostage/terrorist situations suffer a high incidence of acute, chronic, and delayed PTSD in addition to possible medical and surgical injuries. Treatment of these disorders in the acute phase, and even better, preventive measures before symptoms occur, can prevent the development of many chronic or delayed disabilities.

    (1) Task-organized multidisciplinary stress control teams provide mental health treatment services. These teams initiate preventive treatment measures to individuals or groups involved in disasters, terrorist activities, and hostage situations. Teams are task-organized depending upon the number of people involved in the specific incident and the nature of the incident.

    (2) The team assists victims, family members, witnesses, immediate rescuers, and backup medical staff involved in terrorist or hostage situations. A variety of individual and group techniques are used to help return persons to normal functions and to reduce the impact of PTSD. Some examples of these techniques are as follows:

• Professional reassurance of the normality of acute stress reactions and the positive expectation of rapid recovery and coping.

• Critical event debriefing of groups. Everyone is encouraged to talk out what happened and what everyone did (saw, heard, smelled, felt) in detail. In the process, the group corrects misunderstandings and validates and ventilates feelings.

• Individual debriefing as needed.

• Extremely limited use of fast-acting sedating medication in special cases.

• Individual, group, or family follow-up as needed.

d.   Refer to Table 9-4 for some operations other than war mental health recommendations in support of combatting terrorism.

TABLE 9-4. Stress Considerations and Recommendations for Stress Control Issues—Related to Terrorist Attacks

TERRORISM STRESSORS	RECOMMENDATIONS AND ACTIONS
Shock of the event.	Provide honest, accurate information about what actually happened.
Sudden violation of familiar setting.	
Loss of control.	Prevent premature conclusions based on rumors or incomplete data.
Hostile feelings (repressed or expressed).	
Feelings of dependence.	Mediate between needs of the victims and their families, law enforcement, intelligence, and media agencies.
Observation of atrocities.	
Feelings of impotence.	
Regressive behaviors.	
Relocation and isolation responses.	Deploy multidisciplinary stress control team to assist victims, family members, staff, and others involved as rescuers, care givers, and witnesses.
Positive identification with terrorists.	
Sense of being a victim.	
Negative feelings about own country.	
	Debrief in precise detail (group and/or one-on-one).
	Do not overreact to victim's temporary stress reactions.
	Assure of normality of reactions and ability to cope.

9-5. OPERATIONS OTHER THAN WAR (PEACETIME CONTINGENCY OPERATIONS)

These operations are politically sensitive military activities. They are normally characterized by the short-term, rapid projection or employment of forces in operations other than war. They are often undertaken in crisis avoidance or crisis management situations requiring the use of military instruments to enforce or support diplomatic initiatives.

a. *Several Types of Operations.* There are numerous types of operations which are covered by this operational category. In each type of operation, different stress factors will be present. Some operations, such as strikes and raids, inherently involve combat, but are brief. Others, such as peacemaking and noncombatant evacuation operations, run a high risk of violence but under much more ambiguous conditions. Military operations other than war such as peacekeeping, nation building, and disaster relief should not lead to combat, but do involve their own types of stressors. Soldiers are expected to be ambassadors and representatives of the goodwill of the US, yet they may be separated from home or family, sometimes abruptly. They may have to live under uncomfortable or monotonous, boring conditions, perhaps for prolonged periods. In addition, they may be exposed to an entirely different culture whose practices may seem alien, backward, or even repulsive to those who do not understand the historical or practical reasons for them. However, misconduct stress behaviors on the part of our troops can turn local goodwill into enduring resentment and hatred. Table 9-5 provides some of the mental health considerations which may be present in any given peacetime contingency situation and recommended actions which may be taken. Each type of operation is presented below.

b. *Attacks and Raids.* The US conducts attacks and raids for specific purposes other than gaining or holding terrain. Attacks and raids can support rescue and recovery operations. They can destroy or seize equipment or facilities which significantly threaten national security interests. They can also support counter-drug operations by destroying narcotics production or temporary storage facilities used during shipment, or support HN's actions in this regard. Depending on the intensity and duration of combat and on the success (or lack of success), strikes and raids produce traditional combat stress behaviors. The level of secrecy in which the operation is conducted can produce added stress for the soldier and his family. Depending on the size and planned duration of the operation, mental health/combat stress control personnel may accompany the strike force or remain at home station. Mental health/combat stress control personnel should be involved as early as feasible in planning and recovery.

c. *Shows of Force and Demonstrations.* These operations lend credibility to our nation's promises and commitments. They increase our regional influence and demonstrate our resolve to use military force as an instrument of national power. Further, the NCA may order these operations to bolster and reassure friends and allies. Health service support activities to include combat stress control follow the traditional role of providing support to a combat force. Demonstrations may involve high anticipatory anxiety but usually do not cause psychic trauma unless open combat, accidental deaths, or terrorist acts result from them.

d. *Rescue and Recovery Operations.* Rescue and recovery operations are sophisticated actions requiring precise execution, especially when conducted in a hostile environment. These operations may be clandestine or overt. They may include the rescue of US troops or friendly foreign nations, or the location, identification, and recovery of sensitive equipment or items critical to US national security. The level of hostilities to be encountered will vary with each specific mission. Mental health support may be required by the individuals being rescued or the force employed. The level of security for the operation may result in added stressors to those accomplishing the mission.

e. *Disaster Relief Operations.* Disaster relief operations provide emergency assistance to victims of natural and man-made disasters abroad. These operations are responses to requests for immediate help and rehabilitation from foreign governments or international agencies. Mental health support may be required for both victims of the disaster and the military units and health professionals caring for them. The victims' plight may be truly distressing and leave memories of many horrible sights, sounds, and smells for all involved. Recent disasters within the US have also expanded the role of the military (Active and Reserve Components) in domestic disaster relief. In some instances, identification with the victims may even be stronger. For some units, their own families may be involved in the disaster while they must remain on duty for the common good.

f. *Noncombatant Evacuation Operations.* Noncombatant evacuation operations are conducted to relocate civilian noncombatants from locations in a foreign country. These operations are normally conducted to evacuate US citizens whose lives are in danger; however, they may also include the evacuation of HN or third country citizens. These operations are of short duration. They consist of rapidly inserting a force, occupying an objective, and making a planned withdrawal. The amount of force used is normally limited to that required for self-defense and the defense of the operations. Mental health support may be required for both the forces employed and the civilians being evacuated. The need for mental health intervention will depend upon the level of hostilities and the psychological trauma encountered. It also depends on the anticipated duration of the operation and the recent experiences of those being evacuated. After-action debriefing at the small unit level should be routine. All evacuees should receive large group stress debriefing. Critical event debriefings can then be scheduled for such groups who need them.

g. *Operations to Restore Order ("Peacemaking").* These operations are intended to establish and restore peace and order through the use of force. The US conducts these operations when it is in its national interest. Intense efforts are made to stop a violent conflict and to force a return to political and diplomatic methods of resolution. The US typically undertakes "peacemaking" operations at the request of appropriate national authorities in a foreign country. It may also conduct these operations to protect US citizens as part of an international, multilateral, or unilateral operation. The threat of armed resistance or attack by one or more disgruntled parties in the conflict is high. This may take the form of overt battle, major terrorist attack, or covert harassment and sniping. The rules of engagement may require not returning fire until fired upon, with the source of hostile fire clearly identified. Combat stress control support for peacemaking forces requires the traditional support to combat forces. Peacemaking forces must also be prepared to counter added stressors. These stressors may include language and customs barriers, ambiguous threats, and the lack of freedom of movement.

h. *Peacekeeping Operations.* Peacekeeping operations are military operations conducted with the consent of the belligerent parties to a conflict. These operations are conducted to maintain a negotiated truce and to facilitate a diplomatic resolution. The US may participate in peacekeeping operations under the auspices of an international organization, in cooperation with other countries, or unilaterally. Peacekeeping operations support diplomatic efforts to achieve, restore, or maintain peace in areas of potential or actual conflict. Units of peacekeeping forces may use force only in clear cases of self-defense. Due to the nature of peacekeeping operations, misconduct stress behaviors can result from a number of factors. Another characteristic of peacekeeping is isolation of small units for prolonged periods with only radio or telephone contract with their superiors. Also, any violence directed against the peacekeepers will likely come from people whom they intend to be helping. Thus, a sense of betrayal aggravates the stress inherent in the event. Table 9-6 provides mental health considerations and recommendations in support of peacekeeping operations.

  i.   *Humanitarian and Civic Assistance.* US Army combat support/CSS units may be deployed or rotated to friendly HNs to assist that country in developing its resources. These activities serve the basic economic and social needs of the people of the country concerned. They—

  • Support the civilian leadership.

  • Benefit a wide spectrum of the community.

  • Should be self-sustaining (once completed) or supportable by the HN civilian or military agencies. Examples include—

    • Providing medical, dental, and veterinary care in rural areas.

    • Training local health care personnel in hygiene and preventive medicine.

    • Assisting in establishing mental health and social service agencies.

    • Performing engineer projects, such as building roads, bridges, and flood control dams.

Army units engaged in humanitarian and civic assistance range from active Army units deployed for relatively long periods to Reserve Component units on annual training. These conditions can cause a wide variety of stressors related to acclimatization to the environment and culture, coupled with separation from home.

TABLE 9-5. Stress Considerations and Recommendations for Stress Control in Peacetime Contingency Operations

STRESSORS IN PEACETIME CONTINGENCY OPERATIONS	RECOMMENDATIONS AND ACTIONS
Sudden unit deployment.	Develop program for soldiers and families to receive timely information.
Unplanned catastrophe or incident (no textbook solution).	
Small unit activity has great political and media interest.	Develop cohesive unit with strong individual and group problem-solving skills.
Cultural and language differences.	
Lack of freedom of movement.	Improvise as required to accomplish the unit's mission.
Post-traumatic stress of helpers.	
Unclear or misunderstood purpose or mission.	Develop strategy to keep soldiers focused on mission.
Feelings of isolation and frustration.	Implement a sponsorship program for soldiers and families with HN input.
Lack of typical military base operations.	
Inadequate security (the Beirut barracks bombing).	Develop support system to fight isolation.
Excessive security (promotes "bunker mentality").	Implement debriefing process.
Frustration over rules of engagement.	Brief on a regular basis so the unit's mission is understood.
Improper fraternization with local population.	Develop unit goals based on mission priorities.
	Ensure social support system and activities to support cohesion.
	Develop mobile system to support operations.
	Ensure security is consistent with the threat.
	Assure proper behaviors toward local population.

9-6. STRESS PROBLEMS OF MILITARY OPERATIONS OTHER THAN WAR

The stress problems of military operations other than war are recognized by Army long-range planners. The Army must develop an appreciation of low-key, frustrating, and frequently unglorious work. This will not be easy for our soldiers from a culture noted for its impatience and thirst for decisive outcomes. In some areas, we may have to "train down" to less sophisticated equipment because operations other than war frequently are not appropriate for displaying the latest technology. Finally, there is the matter of culture. The American sent to function in an alien culture will have to possess some knowledge of that culture if he is to successfully interact with and influence the members of that culture. For additional information on operations other than war and peacetime contingency operations, refer to FMs 100-5 and 100-20. For specific information on medical operations in this environment, refer to FM 8-42.

TABLE 9-6. Stress Considerations and Recommendations for Stress Control in Peacekeeping Operations

PEACEKEEPING STRESSORS	RECOMMENDATIONS AND ACTIONS
Isolation.	Develop and maintain unit cohesion initiatives.
Boredom.	Job rotation, job cross training.
Cultural alienation.	Trips and recreation in HN.
Repetitious or routine duties.	Job expansion, rigorous training.
Over time, sense of nonsignificant mission.	Continuous emphasis on importance of the mission. Be clear on US role.
As mission continues over the years, increase in fixed facilities versus austerity for soldier on the front line.	Push mobile support packages forward or reduce glamour of fixed facilities in the rear.
Lack of understanding of cultural and political issues of other nations making up peacekeeping force.	Establish effective orientation and cultural exchange programs.
Friction and hostility with other members of the multinational force (usually erupting in off-duty hours).	Positive intramural sports programs and shared activities.
Prejudice or favoritism toward one side in the dispute.	Leadership and education in local history and culture actively promote neutrality and mediation.

CHAPTER 10

WAR AND THE INTEGRATED (NUCLEAR, BIOLOGICAL, AND CHEMICAL) BATTLEFIELD

10-1. INTRODUCTION

War with sustained operations has the potential to generate numerous KIA, WIA, and battle fatigue casualties. To counter this, all units must be well-trained and well-led, and all soldiers made aware of the factors that cause battle fatigue (see Table 10-1). Active prevention programs can reduce the incidence of battle fatigue casualties. Attrited units with exhausted leaders can become incapable of self-help. These units must be permitted to reconstitute psychologically as well as physically. Only then can they be a combat effective force prepared for return to the battle. Battle in the rear area will increase stress and stress casualties in all units.

TABLE 10-1. Likely Stress-Producing Aspects of War on the High-Tech Battlefield

- Brief, high-intensity encounters.
- Extensive casualties in one area, few in another.
- Small units and teams in isolation.
- Soldiers viewing mass destruction and death.
- Unpredictable strikes by long-range weapons.
- Massing of fires in small areas—total destruction evident.

- Soldier reaction to actual use of deadly chemical, biological, and nuclear munitions.
- Loss of most or all of a unit in a matter of seconds or minutes.
- High-tech equipment failure.
- Large numbers of KIA (both military and noncombatants).
- Large numbers of WIA (both military and noncombatants).
- Main roads clogged by noncombatants' vehicles.
- Evacuation system overloaded.
- Unit cohesion challenged by integrating large numbers of new replacement soldiers.
- Existence of rumors, misinformation, or the lack of information.
- Being a lone survivor.
- Continuous operations in chemical and nuclear environments.
- Fighting on unfamiliar or less-familiar terrain.
- High technology (moving and fighting faster than humans can react or maneuver).
- Little guidance on the battlefield versus micromanagement environment of garrison.
- Killed in action and WIA effects will restrict utilization of high-tech equipment. There will be fewer experts remaining.
- Continuing the battle with little information feedback on overall results.
- Continuing offensive push with little chance for rest.
- Moving ahead of logistics tail.

NOTE: At the end of the conflict, after-action debriefings should be conducted. These debriefings, in small groups if possible, are conducted to help prevent PTSD. Post-traumatic stress disorder can occur even in soldiers who showed no disability during combat.

10-2. THE BATTLEFIELDS OF WAR

During war the battlefields are, by definition, chaotic, intense, and highly destructive. They may extend across wider geographical areas. While each of these features can be understood separately, their combined effects constitute the actual setting of operations.

a. *Employment of Soviet-Type Offensive Doctrine.* A characteristic of the offensive doctrine developed by the former Soviet Union is continuous attack by echelons of fresh units. Supported by massed artillery, these units reinforce success, bypass resistance, and break through. All available means are employed, perhaps including NBC, to destroy and disrupt rear area command, control, and logistics. Electronic warfare is another tactic; this blocks communication and spreads misinformation. These tactics maximize confusion, uncertainty, shock, and fatigue. They are intended to make the defender unable to function—to put him in a state of physiologic and mental helplessness. This state was called battle paralysis or shock by the former Soviet Union.

b. *Employment of Battlefield Tactics.* United States Army operations doctrine intends to minimize the effectiveness of potential enemy tactics and turn the tables on an aggressor. Instead of waiting passively to be overrun or isolated, US units must take the initiative and carry the attack to the enemy rear. They must disrupt the enemy's timetable and damage some of his reserve echelons. They must deprive his remaining force of sleep and confidence so they develop battle paralysis or desert their unit. Even with our technological advantage, we must expect to fight around the clock, whether on defense or offense. We must rest and resupply in a highly mobile environment. To succeed, our leaders and troops at all levels must retain the mental agility to detect windows of opportunity in the midst of confusion and stress. Leaders must act spontaneously and synchronously in accordance with their commanders' intent, even though the situation has changed and communications are disrupted. Exhausted and attrited units, even those which have suffered mass casualties, must be returned quickly to the battle. The demands on CSS units, as well as the combat arms, may be extreme. If NBC weapons are employed, the stressors on the integrated battlefield will be incalculably greater.

c. *Lines of Operation.* In modern war, Army forces must prepare to fight campaigns of considerable movement, not only to reduce vulnerability but also to obtain decisive points. The speed with which today's forces can concentrate and the high volumes of supporting fires they can bring to bear will make the intermingling of opposing forces nearly inevitable. Telling friend from foe in darkness, smoke, and dust will be difficult.

NOTE: With the rapid pace and the urgency of firing first, tragic episodes of accidentally killing friendly forces ("brother" killing "brother" or fratricide) may happen. Prevention requires emphasis on vehicle and other identification training, awareness of the tactical situation, and continual risk analysis by leaders at all echelons.

(1) From the first of battle, deep reconnaissance, air mobility, long-range fires, and SOF will blur the distinction between front and rear. This will impose a requirement for all-around defense and self-sufficiency on all units. Throughout the battle area, attack and defense will often take place simultaneously as each combatant attempts to mass, economize locally, and maneuver against his opponent. This creates a state of uncertainty that calls for continued vigilance. Constant vigilance is impossible for individuals to maintain. Only a well-trained highly-cohesive unit can maintain constant vigilance for a prolonged period of time.

(2) Fluidity will also characterize operations in the rear of forward-deployed committed forces. Guerrillas, enemy SOF, and terrorists will seek to avoid set-piece battles and to strike at scattered points of vulnerability. Defending forces will try to preempt such attacks wherever they occur.

d. *Lethal Systems.* With the end of the cold war, sales of high-tech weapons (by the successors to the former Soviet Union and by western countries) may increase rather than decrease. The US intends to maintain our technologic advantage. Potential enemies, however, may field high-quality weapons systems whose range and lethality equal or exceed those of our lead elements. The following examples indicate a concentration of enormous combat power, especially at decisive points. These may be used by potential enemies, as well as by ourselves and our allies.

(1) Potent ground and air systems with missiles (air-to-surface, surface-to-surface, and surface-to-air).

(2) Armored vehicles with reactive armor and all-weather, day-night target acquisition systems.

(3) Multiple-launched rocket systems and tube artillery capable of saturating large areas with fire at really long ranges.

(4) Fixed-wing aircraft and attack helicopters firing multiple bomblet munitions.

(5) Scatterable mines with delayed or smart fuses.

(6) Fuel-in-air explosives which approach the blast effects of low-yield nuclear weapons.

(7) Precision-guided or smart fire and forget munitions.

(8) Nonpersistent or persistent chemical or biological agents, or nuclear warheads.

e.   *Sensors and Communications.* Wide-ranging surveillance, target acquisition sensors, and communications will provide information almost immediately. These will increase the range and scope of battle. Sensors offer the commander more than just timely information on deep enemy locations and activity. They also serve as the basis for attacking enemy follow-on forces or units resting or reconstituting in reserve. Since these attacks can be of vital importance in battle, the sensors and communications means which make them possible are particularly valuable and subject to counterattack. They will also be subjected to electronic countermeasures and deceptive simulation devices which decrease the validity of their input.

NOTE: When functioning, battlefield sensors may contribute to information overload. If too much reliance is placed in them, confusion, stupor, and even panic may occur when they malfunction or are deceived, as they surely will be at times.

Caution should be taken with global position-locating devices. These provide tremendous technologic advantage, but troops must not become so dependent on them that they cannot navigate by map and compass when the device is damaged.

f.   *Command and Control.* The more fluid the battlefield, the more important and difficult it will be to identify decisive points and focus combat power. Under such conditions, it is imperative that the commander's intent and concept of operations be understood throughout the force. Communications will be interrupted by enemy action at critical times. Units will have to fight while out of contact with higher headquarters and adjacent units. Subordinate leaders must be expected to act on their own initiative within the framework of the commander's intent. If soldiers at all levels are trained to be active rather than passive, that in itself will substantially counteract the tendency to become battle fatigue casualties. However, the necessary mental functions are also the functions more likely to deteriorate with sleep loss, fatigue, and stress.

g.   *Air Dimension.* The airspace of a theater is as important a dimension of ground operations as the terrain itself. Airspace is used for maneuver, delivery of fires, reconnaissance and surveillance, transportation, resupply, insertion of forces, patient evacuation, and command and control. The control and use of the air will always affect operations and can decide the outcome of campaigns and battles. Commanders must distribute proportionally air power in planning and supporting their operations. They must protect their own forces from observation, attack, and interdiction by the enemy and must expect the enemy to contest the use of the airspace.

NOTE: • *Having air superiority decreases battle fatigue casualties.*
• *Being subject to air attack increases battle fatigue casualties.*
• *Being hit by friendly air attack greatly increases battle fatigue casualties.*

On the rapidly changing, integrated battlefield, fast-moving friendly aircraft (who are themselves at great risk from air defenses) will have only a split second to distinguish friendly units from enemy targets.

10-3. THE INTEGRATED (NUCLEAR, BIOLOGICAL, AND CHEMICAL) BATTLEFIELD

a.   *The Nuclear, Biological, and Chemical Warfare Threat.* The future battlefield may have a high threat of NBC. Until recently, the former Soviet Union continued to test, produce, and stockpile NBC weapons. Soviet doctrine, organization, training, and equipment supported NBC weapons' use, especially chemical, in order to obtain a military advantage. Former Soviet weapons or design experts may be acquired by Third World countries. Other countries, notably Iraq, have recently used chemical weapons in combat. Use of NBC weapons in rear areas may severely degrade CSS capabilities. Its use would increase casualties and patient work loads, slow operations, and rapidly fatigue personnel because they are forced to operate at the various MOPP levels for extended periods of time. Evacuation and triage will be complicated by contaminated casualties. Vehicles and aircraft will require decontamination at the completion of all missions that encountered contamination from a NBC agent.

b.   *Nuclear Warfare.* Even though the primary purpose of nuclear weapons is to deter their use by others, the threat of nuclear escalation hangs over any military operation involving the armies of nuclear powers. It imposes limitations on the scope and objectives even of conventional operations. United States nuclear weapons may be used only by following specific directives from the NCA after appropriate consultation with allies. Even if such authority is granted, however, the employment of nuclear weapons would be guided more by political and strategic objectives than by the tactical effect. A particular authorized employment of nuclear weapons would certainly magnify the destructiveness of operations and could sharply alter their tempo. Besides the effects of physical damage, the psychological stress on soldiers would be severe, especially if they have not been prepared by their leaders. As a consequence, battles and campaigns may last only hours instead of days or weeks, crippling friendly and enemy combatants.

(1) During the Cold War, a full-scale global exchange of all available thermonuclear weapons was widely believed to be capable of making the earth's environment temporarily unsuited to human civilization. This doom was attributed to persistent radiation and to the dust particles which would be lifted into the upper atmosphere, causing temporary climatic changes and cooling of the earth ("nuclear winter"). More accurate computer models suggest only a partial "nuclear autumn" is likely, but disruption of crops, distribution means, and technologic infrastructure would still cause extreme global suffering.

(2) During the Cold War, many people were convinced that first use of any nuclear weapon in war would inevitably bring on an uncontrollable rapid escalation. The "nuclear winter scenario," however, clearly is not triggered by a small number of low-yield tactical nuclear weapons. Climatic changes were not encountered following the fire-bombing of cities in WWII or the occasional atmospheric testing of large thermonuclear weapons by several of the nuclear powers. The breakup of the Soviet Union and the continued progress in strategic arms limitations makes massive global strikes unlikely now, but the future remains uncertain. Fear of radioactive fallout spreading to other regions of the globe could be created even by a regional nuclear conflict.

(3) Given this background, if US troops know a nuclear weapon has been used but are not being kept adequately briefed by their leaders, some may still think we are on the brink of total world catastrophe and perhaps already over the edge. The spread of rumor will be compounded by the usual problems of communication in the presence of electronic jamming, deliberate misinformation by the enemy, and conventional countermeasures. It may be further disrupted by the electromagnetic pulse of high-altitude nuclear bursts.

(4) Measures must be taken in advance to structure and prepare the soldiers' perceptions of the situation. If this is not done, there is potential for hopelessness. In the common Cold War perception of nuclear war, there was no winner, and even if you survived the initial blast, there is no hope of meaningful survival. It is unknown what such a level of hopelessness for the future of humankind would do to inadequately-trained soldiers. Some soldiers have been exposed to movies, books, and TV shows which have created myths and gross exaggerations about the effects of radiation.

(5) We must prepare soldiers mentally and emotionally for the shock of seeing or hearing a first nuclear attack. An important step is to provide realistic, clearly presented information on the risk of various levels of radiation exposure. Information about true risks, especially low-levels of radiation, should be compared to those risks associated with other commonly accepted hazards. These hazards may include cigarette smoking, therapeutic x-rays, and high altitude flying or residence.

(6) Nuclear weapons use usually implies high-intensity conflict. The possibility of terrorist use (or of attacks on civilian reactors or damage to nuclear-armed weapons in conventional war) must also be considered. United States' forces might be called in as part of a peacekeeping force following use of nuclear weapons. This could be in a conflict between Third World countries or between factions in a civil war within a nuclear power. They might also be called in to support civil authorities following a major nuclear reactor accident. Actions to prepare soldiers for the special stressors of nuclear war are discussed in Appendix A.

c. *Biological Warfare.* The US has renounced the use of biological weapons. However, this unilateral renunciation does not free our own forces from the threat of enemy biological warfare. Army forces must continue to train to fight an enemy who could use biological weapons. New genetic technology may put this capability into the hands of unstable Third World countries (or terrorists) as they develop a pharmaceutical industry. Biological warfare is, therefore, a threat in war and operations other than war (conflicts).

(1) An added stress feature is that it may be difficult to prove that the presence of biological agents is an act of war rather than a natural or accidental occurrence. Reputable biologists still argue that the mycotoxins ("yellow rain") which killed Laotians and Cambodians were not a Soviet (North Vietnamese) weapon but only naturally fermented bee feces (although interestingly, the deaths apparently ceased after the allegations reached the world press coverage). Such weapons could also be used as agents of economic/agricultural sabotage without war being declared. Some of those agents cause long-term contamination of ground and water.

(2) Biological toxins pose a threat similar to chemicals but perhaps harder to defend against. Some toxins, such as the ergot derivatives, produce organic psychotic states. Others, like the mycotoxins, are terror weapons which produce a rapid, horrible death by uncontrollable bleeding.

(3) Infectious organisms create the added hazard (and psychological threat) of contagion and uncontrolled spread. The success of medical science in controlling the rapidly lethal epidemics of his-

tory may make the populace less familiar with how to face this risk. Hence, this unfamiliarity makes the populace more susceptible to panic or maladaptive reactions if newly created threat agents spread more rapidly than defenses can be fielded.

d. *Chemical Warfare.* Chemical warfare was employed in WWII and sporadically since throughout this century. Use of chemical weapons is most likely at the high and low ends of the combat continuum—in high-tech war, or against insurgents or minority groups in remote areas. United States' forces maintain a capability in this area only for deterrence. Chemical warfare presents some of the same complications as nuclear operations, although chemical agents are easier to defend against.

(1) Because chemical weapons are more widespread and the inhibition against their use is lower for some nations, US forces are more likely to face a chemical than a nuclear threat. Chemical weapons are inexpensive and can be produced by Third World countries which have factories that produce fertilizers, insecticides, or pharmaceuticals.

(2) Chemical agents can be lethal and devastating against those who lack adequate protection or training. Nerve agents in sufficient concentration kill within minutes with convulsive seizures. Blister agents rarely kill; rather they are employed as casualty-producing agents. Blister agents like lewisite and mustard can cause either immediate or delayed eye and skin pain, blister formation, and with severe exposure, lung and bone marrow damage. Choking agents cause the lungs to fill with fluid—"drowning on dry land." The potential for mass casualties is great among unprotected troops and civilians. The nature of their deaths, while not more horrible than that from flame, blast, or projectile weapons, has an element of mystery. This may be especially unnerving to those who witness it or come on the scene later.

(3) For troops with adequate protective equipment, chemical agents serve primarily as a harassment which makes other combat and CSS operations much more difficult and time consuming. They also produce high rates of battle fatigue casualties (most of whom return to duty if properly treated) and sublethal chemical injuries (many of which may have long-term disability).

e. *Stress Reaction to the Nuclear, Biological, and Chemical War-fare Threat.* The threat of chemical-biological use will require frequent high levels of MOPP. Using protective clothing and other defensive measures against NBC warfare adds to physical fatigue, primarily because of heat, visual and auditory restriction, and impeded movement. The necessity for precautions will further reduce the time available for rest and sleep, increasing exhaustion. The threat of NBC warfare is a major source of stress whether or not NBC agents are actually used. The associated fear of the unknown, the high degree of ambiguity in detecting the threat, and the uncertain short- and long-term effects of NBC weapons add significant psychological stress to the physical/physiologic stress of MOPP. Stress itself contributes greatly to fatigue.

(1) *Overreaction.* Many soldiers may overreact to an NBC threat—that is, do more than the situation calls for. The reactions listed below were seen in WWI (when chemical weapons were used) and sometimes in WWII (although chemical weapons were not used). They have been seen in peacetime civilian populations, in response to the news about the Three-Mile Island and Chernobyl nuclear reactor accidents, chemical spills, dioxin and toxic chemical waste dumps, and AIDS. Overreaction to NBC are discussed in the following paragraphs.

(a) *Increased sick call (hypochondriasis).* People will over-attend to physical sensations, looking for warning signs. They will find things that worry them and will bring them to the doctor or medic for reassurance or in hope of being sent to safety.

(b) *Increased "conventional" battle fatigue.* Uncertainty, lack of confidence in equipment and leaders, assuming a passive defensive posture, and new or surprise weapons all tend to increase battle fatigue symptoms of anxiety, depression, or simple exhaustion.

(c) *Nuclear, biological, and chemical battle fatigue.* This is battle fatigue with physical symptoms that mimic real NBC injury. The early US Army WWI ratio (in supposedly well-trained but inexperienced troops) was two "gas mania" cases for every one true exposure case (a 2:1 ratio). Epidemic hysteria can occur as the first anxious person hyperventilates (breathes too fast, gets light-headed, and has "pins and needles" sensations and muscle tenseness in face, fingers, and toes). Others, seeing this and believing him to be a true gas casualty, become anxious and hyperventilate, too.

(d) *Malingering.* Nuclear, biological, and chemical battle fatigue is, by definition, not a voluntary behavior. Soldiers who deliberately fake NBC injury, or who self-inflict minor chemical injuries to gain evacuation are malingering, a misconduct stress behavior. Exposing one's radiation counter to radiation artificially in order to raise the count and be relieved of duty also is malingering.

(e) *Panic flight.* This may also be epidemic. It occurs when a group feels threatened, unprepared, and believes that the only defense is immediate flight. Some event causes one soldier to run, after which the others in the group panic and run wildly.

(f) *Rumor.* The former Soviet Union, through their military literature, recognized and valued the threat of NBC warfare to "demoralize through rumor." These rumors were concerned with family and home, as well as with self and unit, in any perceived NBC war. Commanders must counsel the spreaders of rumor and ensure that the best available information passes through the chain of command and reaches every soldier. Covering up or withholding information can permanently destroy the leadership's credibility. Utilization of unit or attached public affairs personnel and a solid Command Information Program (CIP) can prevent rumors or stop them from spreading. A wide range of CIP products are available through public affairs channels. Commanders should avail themselves of these.

(g) *Excessive anxiety and "phobic" avoidance.* Soldiers may refuse to go into places or to use equipment which is wrongly believed to be contaminated. Even when they go, they may be too anxious and cautious to perform well. They may shun people who are believed to be contagious or contaminated.

(h) *Excessive decontamination ("obsessive-compulsive" cleaning).* This wastes time and scarce supplies. This can even cause dermatologic problems if soldiers use caustic decontamination chemicals on their skin.

(i) *Congregating in safe areas.* People will naturally find excuses to stay in collective protection or safe areas. Headquarters personnel in such protection areas may get out of touch with the troops in the field. Medical teams which must work in collective protection areas may find many nonpatients giving reasons to join those who are working inside and being difficult to move out. The misconduct stress behavior version of this is desertion to hide in safe areas.

(j) *Stealing protective equipment.* If there is not enough protective equipment or collective protection to go around, another potential misconduct stress behavior is stealing from or killing others to take over their protection.

(k) *Suspiciousness.* Vision and hearing are impaired in MOPP and everyone looks alike. Even friends may not be readily identified. People tend to develop a "paranoid" suspicion of the strange, monster-like figures; they may become jumpy and shoot at shapes or sounds without checking first. This requires emphasis on vehicle and other target identification training, challenge procedures, and passwords. Identifying labels may have to be added to personalize the MOPP gear.

(l) *Risks to leaders.* Mission-oriented protective posture requires much more active leadership. It hides the usual nonverbal cues of alertness, understanding, and readiness to act which leaders normally rely on. Leaders must move around, touch to get attention, and insist on information and confirmation. This movement increases the leader's risk of heat exhaustion, carelessness, and being accidentally shot by a jumpy soldier. Accidental fratricide (killing of leaders and other friendly personnel) has been alarmingly high in MOPP field exercises which use the multiple integrated laser engagement simulation deices. The same problem occurs in jungle and night fighting where vision and hearing are also reduced. Fratricide must be prevented by careful adherence to the TSOP, coordination between units, target identification, and the use of challenge procedures.

(m) *Isolation and loss of cohesion.* Mission-oriented protective postures interfere with normal friendly support, such as conversation, sharing snacks, or simply smiling. As a result of the sensory and social isolation and encapsulation, soldiers tend to feel alone. They may feel surrounded by a totally hostile world in which even the air they breathe is against them. This isolation tends to make people become passive, insecure, and at high risk for battle fatigue unless it is actively counteracted. It requires a more active, verbal, and deliberate effort to maintain a sense of comradeship and unit cohesion.

(2) *Underreactions.* Underreactions may be more likely than overreactions in some situations.

(a) *Denial.* Things are too horrible for a soldier to think about, so he just thinks about something else.

(b) *Rationalization.* "No one would be so crazy as to use such terrible weapons, so why should we waste our time preparing and training for them?"

(c) *Fatalism.* "If anyone is so crazy as to use these weapons, they are so terrible that I can't protect myself anyway, so why bother to prepare, and train?"

(d) *False alarm.* If there is a threat situation with frequent false alarms, troops may neglect alerts and fail to react, believing it "just another false alarm" when, in fact, it is the real thing.

(e) *Overconfidence.* "We have this one defense (or detector, or higher headquarters, or whatever) that's going to warn and protect us. We can forget about everything else."

(f) *"Pie in the sky."* "The Strategic Defense Initiative, or immunization, or something will solve all these problems within the next year, so why train now?"

(g) *Intellectualism.* "This is so serious that we have to study it and do more research before we take any action to correct the problem."

(3) *Consequences of the maladaptive responses.* Any of these maladaptive responses lowers the maximum advantage that protective equipment and training can provide during accomplishment of the mission. Underreactions may lead to discarding equipment and failure to follow the TSOP. Overreactions tend to disrupt a unit's overall ability to perform its mission. Appendix A presents recommendations for how leaders can prevent or correct these maladaptive reactions to the NBC threat.

CHAPTER 11

PREVENTION OF BATTLE FATIGUE CASUALTIES AND MISCONDUCT STRESS BEHAVIORS

11-1. INTRODUCTION

In combat, battle fatigue is inevitable but high battle fatigue casualty rates are not. History shows that highly trained and cohesive units with good leadership have had fewer than one such casualty for every ten WIA, even in intensely heavy fighting. This is significantly fewer than the usual one per four or five in moderate-intensity battle and one per two or three in intense fighting. By knowing what factors in the tactical and overall situation increase battle fatigue, leaders and unit members can take action to counteract those factors. They must share the burden, resolve internal conflicts, build unit cohesion, and reduce stress. The same measures, plus positive adherence to discipline and the Law of Land Warfare, also prevent misconduct stress behaviors which could defeat the purpose of the mission. We can overcome the stressors of the battlefield—

• Through tough, realistic training which builds confidence.

• By looking out for each other.

11-2. LEADER'S ROLE IN TRAINING BATTLE FATIGUE PREVENTION

a.   History shows what kinds of situations and stressors tend to produce battle fatigue casualties. Some are conditions which can be modified or controlled by good leadership. Other situations or events may be beyond the leader's control; however, knowing which situations or events increase stress and battle fatigue enables the leader to compensate by reducing other stressors and taking corrective actions. The leader must also plan for the care of battle fatigue casualties and still accomplish the mission.

b. Mental health/combat stress control personnel have the mission to give formal training and consultation on how to reduce stressors. This training and consultation is provided to both medical and line officers, NCOs, chaplains, and troops.

c. Appendix E elaborates on material which is part of the Advanced NCO Course and Advanced Officer Course core curricula. The same material is also outlined in GTAs 21-3-4, -5, and -6. These GTAs are designed to facilitate "hip pocket training" in the field. They are camouflaged pocket cards which should be available through all Army Support Centers. The GTAs can serve as training aids in peacetime and as reminders and checklists in war.

11-3. WHAT THE MEMBERS OF THE UNIT CAN DO TO CONTROL STRESS

a. Unit leaders and members can control stress by assisting one another. They need to be able to recognize stress in each other. One important way in which stress can be alleviated is by talking things out ("ventilation"). This requires encouragement and listening to the soldier under stress. Realistic reassurance is helpful. Arguing with the soldier and being critical or disparaging usually is not helpful. Ways which unit leaders and members can assist one another in controlling stress may include—

• All soldiers being assigned or developing "battle buddies" with whom they share their feelings and ventilate about their experiences.

• Officers and NCOs in the same unit encouraging each other to talk things out together; especially those issues or feelings they cannot share with their troops.

• Officers and NCOs in sister units providing ventilation for each other.

• Officers and senior NCOs in the chain of command, chain of support, and staff positions encouraging junior leaders to talk freely about their feelings at suitable times and places without fear of reprisal. Formal after-action debriefings of the unit leaders after difficult actions are one example of suitable times. Another example is during change of command transition workshops.

• The unit chaplain being someone that anyone can ventilate to about anything.

b. Should a unit member be in a crisis, a number of actions may be useful. These actions are to—

• Observe and attempt to calm the soldier.

• Protect him from danger (restrain only if necessary).

• Ensure that someone takes charge of the situation, finds out what is going on, and takes appropriate action. Specific actions which should be taken by a buddy or junior leader are outlined in GTA 21-3-4 and -5.

11-4. WHAT THE INDIVIDUAL CAN DO TO CONTROL COMBAT STRESS

a. Individuals must drink enough fluids, eat enough food, and attempt to get rest/sleep as often as possible.

b. Everyone should learn at least two relaxation techniques (and preferably more) that can be used at times when physical exercise is not feasible.

• One technique should provide quick reduction of excessive alertness without taking the mind, eyes, or hands off the task.

• A second technique should provide deep relaxation for refreshing sleep even under high-stress situations.

c. Care must be taken to use relaxation techniques only at tactically appropriate times. Mental health personnel can assist in teaching these methods. Useful techniques which can be used alone or in combination include—

• Visual imaging self-relaxation. Imagine yourself in a relaxing situation. Pick your own relaxing situation, then imagine it with every sense of your body—colors, shapes, textures, sounds, smells, temperature, and touch of it.

• Brief or progressive muscular relaxation. Tense your muscles for a few seconds (approximately 5-10) and then slowly release this tension while feeling the warm and heavy sensation that occurs when you relax. Either tense all your muscles at once or start with the muscles in your toes and work slowly up the muscles in the rest of your body.

• Stretching. Stretch your muscles and joints, move them around, and shake out the tension.

★   ★   ★

CAUTION
When the soldier must stay alert and be responsive to the environment, special relaxation techniques can be used that will not disrupt performance. In such situations, deep relaxation techniques would be tactically inappropriate and unsafe.

★   ★   ★

• Positive self-talk. Say to yourself, "Easy does it," "Take your time," "I can do it," "OK, go for it!" or any other brief words of encouragement.

• Abdominal breathing. Breathe slowly and deeply, using the abdominal muscles (not the chest muscles) to move the air in and out. Even one slow breath in which you breathe in, hold for 2-3 seconds, and then exhale slowly (about 5 seconds) can steady the nerves and refocus attention.

• Breathing meditation. Focus your attention on your breathing, especially each time you breathe out. Say the same word or short phrase once each time you exhale (such as the word "one" or "relax"), over and over, while passively letting all other thoughts drift out of your mind.

d.   Individuals should share feelings constructively ("ventilation").

e.   Individuals can also reduce stress by planning ahead, preparing for the mission, and ensuring readiness. The best way to alleviate stress is to take appropriate action. The above techniques should be practiced frequently until they become automatic.

11-5. PREVENTION OF MISCONDUCT STRESS BEHAVIORS

The measures which reduce battle fatigue and prevent battle fatigue casualties should also help reduce the incidence of misconduct stress behaviors. However, additional actions also need to be practiced consistently by leadership at all echelons and by buddies at the small unit level.

a.   Clearly state and teach the Standards of Conduct. United States forces will faithfully adhere to the Law of Land Warfare and the UCMJ.

b.   Reemphasize those standards repeatedly, especially every time they are violated by the enemy or at the first early signs of slippage by our troops. Some of the early signs may include talking about breaking the law, stretching the interpretation, or committing acts in the "gray" areas which cannot be documented for legal action. Let troops express (ventilate) their frustrations verbally among themselves, but not in action.

c.   Emphasize national, Army, and unit pride in living by the standard even under provocative conditions. "We are American soldiers of the (unit). I know how you feel, but we do not do that stuff. Those who do have let us down and are no longer part of us."

d.   Explain, as often as necessary, the ethical, legal, practical, and tactical reasons why we obey the rules. For example, "Provoking us to commit atrocities is exactly what the enemy is trying to do to achieve his objectives, not ours." Restate the mission and its objectives clearly.

e.   Clearly state and consistently enforce the rules and regulations against substance abuse, fraternization, and misconduct. Develop a group sense of "family" that makes such improper behavior morally and spiritually unacceptable as well as illegal and punishable.

f.   Set the personal example of correct conduct.

g.   Report all violations.

h.   Prosecute all verifiable violations.

i.   Consistently and fairly punish misconduct and violation of the UCMJ in peacetime to set the standard that misbehavior will not be tolerated.

LEADER ACTIONS TO OFFSET BATTLE FATIGUE RISK FACTORS

This appendix provides recommendations for how leaders can control situations or events that cause battle fatigue. Table A-1 summarizes the risk factors that are discussed.

TABLE A-1. Summary (Risk Factors)

I. HOME FRONT (A-1)

RISK FACTOR: Problems and uncertainties on the home front.
LEADER ACTION: Stabilize the home front.
- Help families develop unit identity and a support system.
- Reduce problems of a rapid mobilization and deployment.
- Prepare families in the theater of operations for the noncombatant evacuation operation (NEO) plan.

II. NEW SOLDIER (A-2)

RISK FACTOR: Soldier is new in the unit.
LEADER ACTION: Promote unite cohesion.
- Ensure new arrivals are welcomed into the group.
- Impart unit pride and identity.
- Keep members of the same small teams always working together when possible.
- Encourage unit-centered social interaction.
- Bring the whole unit together.
- Conduct small team after-action debriefings after every rugged action.

III. FIRST EXPOSURE (A-3)

RISK FACTOR: First exposure to a major combat stressor.

LEADER ACTION: Conduct tough, realistic training.

- Build soldiers' confidence.
- Seek out challenging and difficult environments for training (train as you will fight).
- Emphasize that the result should be success.

IV. UNIT CASUALTIES (A-4)

RISK FACTOR: Casualties in the unit.

LEADER ACTION: Prepare the unit to endure battle losses.

- Talk frankly and prepare for the possibility of casualties, both WIA and KIA.
- Practice casualty care and evacuation routinely.
- Conduct memorial services.

V. PASSIVE POSTURE, DEFENSELESS TO ATTACK, OR HIT BY FRIENDLY FIRE (A-5)

RISK FACTOR: Under attack and unable to strike back.

LEADER ACTION: Train troops in active defense against these threats.

- Prepare units for the experience of being bombarded.
- Train in active defensive tactics.
- Drill to prevent friendly fire casualties.

VI. IMMOBILITY (A-6)

RISK FACTOR: Immobility during static, heavy fighting.

LEADER ACTION: Recognize static, heavy fighting and institute protective measures.

- Rotate units back to reserve positions so they can move freely.
- Keep the units informed.
- Provide the best possible support for water, food, clothing, and mail.

VII. LACK OF INFORMATION/SUPPORT (A-7)

RISK FACTOR: Lack of information and failure of expected support.

LEADER ACTION: Keep information flowing.

- Keep yourself informed.
- Keep all the troops informed.

VIII. NUCLEAR, BIOLOGICAL, AND CHEMICAL WEAPONS (A-8)

RISK FACTOR: High threat of NBC weapons use and actual use.

LEADER ACTION: Prepare troops for NBC threat contingencies.

- Keep information flowing and control rumors.
- Emphasize that our intention is deterrence.
- Put NBC (especially chemical) defense in realistic perspective in terms of protection.
- Practice flexible MOPP procedures.
- Emphasize buddy aid by those in MOPP rather than self-administration of antidotes.
- Have buddies in MOPP administer antidotes to fellow soldiers.
- Reduce ambiguity by having unit TSOP that is adaptable to mission scenarios.
- Train in the protective mask often.
- Conduct training at different MOPP levels as often as possible.
- Use mask confidence exercises to build confidence.
- Emphasize routine procedures and professionalism.
- Make field training exercises realistic.
- Train hard, and be prepared to manage mild heat stress in well-acclimatized, fit soldiers.

IX. DEPRIVED OF SLEEP (A-9)

RISK FACTOR: Sleep loss.

LEADER ACTION: Practice sleep discipline and sleep planning.

- Set shifts whenever possible.
- Give all soldiers at least 4 hours uninterrupted sleep (or 5 hours, if interrupted) each 24 hours if shifts are impractical.
- Identify critical tasks which are vulnerable to the effects of sleep loss.
- Practice counterfatigue measures.

X. PHYSICALLY RUN-DOWN (A-10)

RISK FACTOR: Run-down physical condition.

LEADER ACTION: Protect the physical well-being of the troops.

- Ensure the best water, food, equipment, shelter, and sanitation (and sleep) possible.
- Explain why the hardship is necessary.

XI. INADEQUATE FITNESS (A-11)

RISK FACTOR: Lack of physical fitness.

LEADER ACTION: Assure physical fitness.

XII. OLDER VETERAN OR SHORT-TIMER (A-12)

RISK FACTOR: Cumulative combat exposure or "being short."

LEADER ACTION: Recognize and manage the "older veteran" or "short-timer" syndrome.

- Maintain a rotation plan which avoids relieving soldiers of duties prematurely without keeping them so long they become ineffective.
- Avoid a policy of relieving "short" soldiers from dangerous missions during their final weeks.
- Do give a period of minimal danger for "short soldiers" just before the soldier's departure.

A-1. HOME FRONT

a. *Risk Factor:* Problems and uncertainties on the home front.

(1) Worrying about what is happening back home distracts soldiers from focusing their psychological defenses on the combat stressors. It creates internal conflict over performing their combat duty and perhaps not surviving to resolve the uncertainties at home. An Israeli Defense Force study conducted after the 1973 Yom Kippur War found concerns about the home front to be the strongest predictive factor which distinguished between soldiers who became "battle shock" casualties and those who were decorated for heroic acts.

(2) The home front problem may be a negative one—marital or financial problems, illness, uncertain job security (if a reservist); or it may be something positive—newly married, new baby. All soldiers face greater potential problems and uncertainties with personal matters if the military conflict is not popular at home.

b. *Leader Actions.* Stabilize the home front.

(1) Help families develop unit identity and a support system.

- Involve the soldiers' families in unit social activities. Teach them about the unit's mission and history and include them in the sense of unit cohesion.

- Know soldiers' personal backgrounds as well as their military skills. Keep notes to remember details about each soldier's spouse, children, parents, and outside interests which you can learn.

• Help soldiers and their families to use Army and civilian support services such as Army Community Service, Army Emergency Relief, post morale/welfare/recreation activities, and the Red Cross.

• Encourage soldiers and their families to draw moral support and assistance from the unit and its members.

• Use the unit or post chaplains and mental health team as valuable resources. Get to know them personally, and encourage soldiers and families to talk with them when they can help. Make command referrals to mental health when necessary.

• Promote and support a unit family or spouse network (family support group) which communicates information and provides emotional support and guidance for practical assistance to every unit family. Include those who live far from the unit's military post on the mail-out roster for disseminating information about the unit.

(2) Reduce problems of rapid mobilization and deployment for Active Component and Reserve Component soldiers. This turmoil must be reduced by prior planning which has been communicated to and practiced with the family. Help soldiers prepare themselves and their families for the disruption and stress of a rapid deployment.

• Establish a system which keeps family members informed about the progress of the deployment and the health and safety of their spouses, consistent with realistic security restrictions.

• Encourage family members to participate in family action plan or community action plan conferences.

• Encourage commanders to conduct periodic feedback sessions for families.

• Assure rapid humane casualty reporting to families and provide assistance to them.

• Involve families in organizing the unit's welcome home party.

(3) Prepare families in the theater of operations for the NEO plan. Soldiers will have great emotional stress moving out to their combat positions and keeping their minds focused on their missions if they are not confident that someone they trust is looking after their families in the best way the situation allows. Failure to provide that

reassurance runs a high risk of battle fatigue casualties and of misconduct stress behaviors such as going AWOL to stay with the families.

• Have a credible NEO plan; talk about it and practice it.

• Have a credible contingency plan for what will be done if the NEO plan cannot be implemented because of political or operational reasons. Talk about that frankly, and practice the contingency plan, too. Someone who is known and trusted must be left in charge of those families.

• Make clear to the soldiers that the best way they can protect their families is by doing their combat duty.

A-2. NEW SOLDIER

a. *Risk Factor.* Soldier is new in the unit.

(1) The new soldier has not yet established trust and cohesion with buddies and leaders. The Israeli study, discussed above, found this to be the second strongest predictor distinguishing battle shock casualties from decorated heroes.

(2) New replacements who have no prior combat experience are at special risk because not only are they facing extreme stress for the first time, but also the veteran soldiers have little basis on which to trust them. Veteran soldiers who are coming to a new unit after recovering from a wound or as survivors from other units are also at risk. These veterans may adapt quicker than the new replacements, provided they do not have internal conflicts and too much unresolved battle fatigue.

(3) Soldiers who have been given increased/new job responsibilities, such as just being promoted to NCO, are at risk. These soldiers may also be under special stress for a while as they adjust to no longer being "one of the old gang" and develop new horizontal bonding with other NCOs.

(4) Building unit cohesion is extremely important. The most important motive which keeps soldiers doing their duty in combat is personal bonding. Personal bonding is the personal trust and loyalty among members of a small unit. This bonding makes them prefer to stick together in exceedingly stressful situations, even when great hardship and danger are present.

• The leader needs to encourage as much unit cohesion as possible. (See FM 22-100.) The leader ensures that the personal bonding is strengthened by a sense of the unit's military identity (esprit) and its mission.

• This combination of unit esprit and personal bonding makes "unit cohesion."

• Unit esprit is like concrete; it keeps its shape, but shatters easily.

• Personal bonding alone is like steel wire mesh; it is hard to break but easy to bend.

• Combining the two produces a result that is far stronger than the sum of its parts. Unit cohesion is like reinforced concrete. It neither bends nor breaks.

• Working together to overcome danger and survive is, in itself, a good way to produce fast cohesion. But there are two disadvantages in waiting until the danger is close before starting to develop unit cohesion.

• First, there is the big risk that the danger and stress will break up the insufficiently cohesive team and roll over it. Everyone will simply get killed or develop total battle fatigue.

• Second, it is possible to develop personally cohesive groups who care only about their own comfort and survival and not about the mission.

b.   *Leader Actions:* Promote unit cohesion.

(1) Ensure that new arrivals are welcomed into the group and become known and trusted members quickly.

• In-brief the soldier explaining what the standards are and tell him how the unit has performed in terms of meeting its own standards.

• Appoint a suitable sponsor for each newcomer and monitor to see that the sponsor shows the newcomer around and assists him in settling in on the job and in the community.

• Introduce new personnel (formally or informally) to all unit members.

• Link the new soldier with an appropriate buddy or buddies in the combat zone. This is essential for proper orientation.

• Give newcomers time, if possible, to develop combat attitudes, skills, and cohesion over several days before putting them into extremely stressful or critical situations.

• Conduct formidable, meaningful combat training whenever possible, involving both the new and the veteran soldiers together.

(2) Impart unit pride and identity.

• Educate the soldiers regarding the history of the small unit, its parent units, the branch of service, and the Army.

• Tell stories which honor and illustrate historical examples of soldiers and units (as much like yours as possible) who showed initiative, endurance and resilience, who bounced back from defeat, who overcame heavy odds, or whose self-sacrifice led to eventual triumph of the higher cause ("Remember the Alamo!"). Do not just tell about easy military or small unit successes.

• Establish training criteria which will challenge each soldier or each member of a team, squad, platoon, and company. These criteria should be recognized as significant common challenges that all must pass.

• Use distinctive unit symbols, tokens, and awards (such as patches, plaques, and coins) which must be earned. Informal citations and distinctions can also be extremely meaningful.

3) Keep members of the same small teams always working together with their leader.

• Assign details and projects to a team, and let its leader organize how they will be done.

• Send a group, small teams, or at least buddy pairs if there is an opportunity for R&R. Do not send a collection of individuals who will not work together in the future.

• Use equipment drills, physical fitness exercises, and team sports to promote mutual reliance and closeness within each team and positive competition and respect among all teams. These activities let off steam, prevent boredom, and help integrate new replacements during times of low mission activity.

• Praise and reward teams, as well as the individual members, for their performance.

• Use team-building techniques—have team members set team goals. Conduct team rap sessions to talk about what is going well and not so well in the group. Encourage open, honest communication.

4) Encourage unit-centered social interaction outside duty hours. Monitor these activities to—

• Prevent drug or alcohol abuse (which tense soldiers may want to use to "unwind").

• Prevent fraternization (within the chain of supervision; between officers, NCOs, and enlisted; between persons who are married to others, and so forth).

• Discourage cliques or interest groups which exclude or pick on other unit members.

(5) Bring the whole unit together, when the situation permits.

• Conduct formations, meals, award ceremonies, and other formal or informal occasions which let the teams (squads, platoons, and/or companies) get to know the members of the other teams.

• Conduct activities which let individuals see the whole unit working together.

c. *Leader Actions:* Conduct small team after-action debriefings after every difficult action (in training and in combat). An after-action debriefing is an extension of after-action reviews which are routing in training. Reconstruct what really happened so that the team benefits from the lessons learned. At the same time, this releases bottled-up emotions and inner conflict that can lead to decreased unit cohesion, battle fatigue, and perhaps even to PTSD. This is the purpose of the after-action debriefing. Feelings of anger and mistrust may go away on their own once the soldier sees how things looked to the others. At least the feelings are out in the open and can be dealt with honestly. Soldiers' natural emotions of loss and grief come out, too, when buddies are wounded or killed in combat. Guilt or shame may come out when soldiers make mistakes. Such soldiers can be comforted and helped to put things into perspective by the rest of the team. The mistakes can be acknowledged and forgiven or atoned for. When conducting the after-action debriefing, the leader must—

(1) Select a location that is relatively safe from enemy attack.

(a) Ensure the location has adequate comfort and enough light to see everyone.

(b) Bring the team (squad, crew, and/or section) together when the situation permits and while the events are still fresh in their minds.

(c) Include only those personnel who took part in the action.

NOTE: Exceptions for permitting others may include unit members or new replacements who just missed the action. Also, personnel that the team trusts, such as the medic or the chaplain, may be included.

(2) Set the ground rules.

(a) State that the purpose of the after-action debriefing is not to find fault or fix blame. The purpose is to share the experience as a team, to strengthen the team, and to talk and learn together how to do better.

(b) Allow all ranks to freely express their observations and opinions openly and honestly without fear of ridicule or reprisal from their peers or leaders. No verbal abuse or fighting is allowed.

(c) Ensure all personnel agree that personal information, feelings, and reactions which others share within the session will be privileged information and not be talked about outside the group with anyone.

(d) State that operational lessons learned or system problems which the debriefing identifies will be shared with other units or up the chain of command or the NCO chain of support. Such lessons and issues will be worded in terms that do not identify the specific team, unit, and individuals involved.

NOTE: Make clear that these ground rules do not exempt the leaders and soldiers in the team from upholding and defending the UCMJ and the Law of Land Warfare.

(e) Ensure personnel know their rights if the event being debriefed involved potentially illegal acts or misconduct stress behavior. Each individual, and the team as a whole, has an obligation to do the right thing; however, their individual rights must be protected. The team may wish to involve a chaplain or legal counsel in the debriefing or in a subsequent group session.

(3) Reconstruct the action from everyone's memories.

(a) Start just before the beginning of the action with the first person that was involved.

(b) Ask about facts and details to get a clear picture.

(c) Bring in others as they joined the action.

(d) Provide the opportunity for everyone to retell what he saw and did so that the big picture can be seen and agreed upon by everyone.

(e) Make a special effort to involve those who are silent and seem not to want to talk, but do not require anyone to speak.

(4) Share thoughts and reactions to the action.

(a) Do not ask specifically about emotions and feelings or force anyone to talk about them if he does not want to.

(b) Wait until the facts are clear, then ask about the thoughts that came to their minds during the action.

(c) Ask what were their reactions to those thoughts.

(d) Allow feelings to come out naturally, either in words or in the tone of voice, facial expression, body posture, or even tears. The feelings should then be acknowledged and validated by the leader and the rest of the team. This will encourage others to be more open about their feelings.

(e) Keep this a positive learning experience in which natural human emotions and mistakes, however painful or "bad," are accepted as natural but controllable.

(f) Prevent scapegoating or isolation of individual soldiers.

(5) Encourage talk about any physical or mental sign of battle fatigue anyone may be having if the action was a high stress event.

(a) Remind personnel that battle fatigue signs are a normal reaction.

(b) Ensure personnel that the battle fatigue signs normally improve with time and talk.

(6) Bring the focus back to the mission after the feelings have been recognized and ventilated.

(a) Expand on the mission.

(b) Encourage talk on what was learned and how to do it better the next time.

(c) Review what went well and the positive things that were accomplished.

(7) Use after-action debriefings to orient new unit members. These debriefings familiarize them with the unit's most recent history, introduce them to the veterans' roles and personalities, and acquaint them with the unit's TSOP. It also helps when merging survivors of two units into one, with or without other new replacements.

A-3. FIRST EXPOSURE

a. *Risk Factor:* First exposure to a major stressor.

(1) The first exposure to a significant stressor is usually a time of high stress and risk of battle fatigue. Likewise, it is inevitable when a unit or individual first encounters true combat with its extreme noise, confusion, wounding of soldiers, and violent death. Tough, realistic training helps, but no training can fully equal the real consequences of kill-or-be-killed. The shock will also be intense for medical personnel, even in rear area hospitals, unless they have had extensive emergency room experience.

(2) Even experienced troops may suffer increased battle fatigue when confronted with a surprise enemy weapon, tactic, or attack. Examples include the following:

• The first exposure to tanks and gas in WWI.

• German blitzkrieg tactics with Stuka aircraft, the "88" anti-tank gun, and later the "Screaming Meemie" mortar.

• Improved conventional munitions and napalm bombs (Israel against Egypt, US against North Vietnam) and wire-guided anti-tank missiles (Egypt and Syria against Israel).

• Strange, hostile terrain and climate. This type stressor can demoralize even experienced units. (At first, a crack Australian division suffered severe stress casualties when suddenly transferred from the desert of North Africa to the jungle of New Guinea.)

b. *Leader Actions:* Conduct rugged, realistic training.

(1) Build soldiers' confidence in their own ability, their lead-

ership, and their equipment, initially through rugged, realistic training, and later through success on the battlefield.

• Tough means hard work and continuous operations even during inclement weather conditions.

• Realistic means as similar to the combat mission and combat environment as possible, including the noise, smoke, dust, confusion, delays, setbacks, casualties, and simulated danger and sights.

(2) Seek out challenging and difficult environments for training to increase the unit's skills and confidence. The purpose is not learning to suffer. The objectives of this training are twofold:

• First, learn to accomplish the mission in spite of suffering.

    • Build toughness, tolerance to discomfort, and the confidence that we can take it and do the job.

    • Perform essential tasks for mission accomplishment while adapting to combat and defending against enemy attack.

• Second, learn how to suffer as little as possible.

    • Know how to take care of yourself and each other so that everyone comes through "OK," even though the conditions are stressful.

    • Educate the soldiers to maintain themselves, each other, and the equipment as a matter of professional pride and personal caring, rather than just as discipline. Explain why it is important, not just picky details.

(3) Emphasize that the ultimate result should be success.

(4) Use tough training to achieve specific objectives:

• Learn each soldier's strengths and weaknesses.

• Maximize soldier's strengths while learning how to minimize his weaknesses.

• Identify which are the truly key combat mission tasks. These are given training emphasis. However, remember that some unglamorous things like preventive maintenance and resupply can be truly critical.

• Identify the best qualified soldiers to perform those key tasks. Individuals do differ in training, adaptability, and ability to learn under stress.

• Cross-train! There must be several people capable of doing every key task, including leader tasks and yours.

A-4. UNIT CASUALTIES

a. *Risk Factor:* Casualties in the unit.

• Soldiers in the unit being killed and wounded is the strongest indicator of "combat intensity" and usually is accompanied by increased battle fatigue casualties. This is especially true if many casualties occur in a short time.

• Heavy casualties naturally shake soldiers' confidence in their own chance of survival. The impact is strongest if losses are in the soldiers' own small unit. Loss of a trusted leader or close buddy is both an emotional shock and a threat to unit integrity and survival. New replacements are an unknown quantity who may not know the TSOP and cannot yet be fully relied upon. Losses naturally arouse the battle fatigue symptoms of reduced confidence, feeling exposed and abandoned, and perhaps guilt, anger, and mistrust.

• These feelings will be magnified if the soldier does not feel that everything feasible was done to care for and evacuate the wounded and that respect for the dead was not shown. Confidence in the health service support system can help compensate for the fear of being wounded.

b. *Leader Actions:* Prepare the unit to endure battle losses.

(1) Talk frankly and prepare for the possibility of casualties in the unit and of team members being killed.

• Talk in the unit about possible loss of leaders and unit members. It will happen in war (even in CSS units) and must not come as a surprise.

• Train junior leaders to take over when senior leaders need sleep or if they become casualties.

• Keep the junior leaders as continuously informed as possible so that they can assume command on short notice without missing stride.

• Cross-train soldiers so that every key task can be performed proficiently by several soldiers.

(2) Routinely practice casualty care and evacuation.

• Train everyone on basic lifesaving self-aid/buddy aid. Select the best soldiers for additional combat lifesaver training, one for every team or crew. Practice this routinely.

• Practice realistic use of any assigned medical personnel and evacuation of casualties as part of any combat exercise. If you can occasionally get moulage kits to make soldiers appear to have serious battle wounds, this will help to harden your soldiers to better face some of the sights of battle.

• Practice self-aid/buddy aid techniques for battle fatigue.

(3) Conduct the small team after-action debriefings after any losses (in training and in combat).

(4) Conduct memorial services for the unit's dead. This will help the soldiers in grieving, provided the service is done with sensitivity.

• While a unit chaplain may play an important role in this service, the commander and junior leaders should be the main participants.

• The dead soldier's friends and others who knew the soldier personally should have an active part in planning the services, as well as special roles in the ceremony. All ideas should receive equal consideration.

5) Plan ahead for a rapid, positive integration of new personnel.

A-5. PASSIVE POSTURE, DEFENSELESS TO ATTACK, OR HIT BY FRIENDLY FIRE

a.   *Risk Factor:* Under attack and unable to strike back.

• Indirect (artillery) fire usually causes more battle fatigue casualties in relation to killed and wounded than does direct fire. This is partly because of the massed, impersonal destruction that a barrage can cause.

• Even more, it is because the troops feel themselves helpless victims of pure chance. Armor and air attacks also tend to produce disproportionate battle fatigue casualties in troops who are not trained to shoot back, such as rear area support units.

• In WWII, many battle fatigue casualties were attributed to the troops' perception that German tanks, "88" artillery, and other weapons were far better than our own, so that we did not have a fair chance to strike back.

• In operations other than war (conflicts), similar frustration is produced by hidden snipers who fire from areas where return fire is limited by the rules of engagement. It may be caused by mines and booby traps and by combatants who cannot be distinguished from the civilians one is supposed to protect. However, this is more likely to trigger misconduct stress behaviors than battle fatigue.

b. *Leader Actions:* Train troops in active defense against these threats.

(1) Prepare units for the experience of being bombarded.

• Expose all troops in training to the sights and sounds of heavy artillery or air attack impacting at close range. This can be done in suitably safe bunkers, ideally with live artillery fire, but if that is unfeasible, with pyrotechnics and sound effects.

• Explain to the troops that dug-in but inexperienced troops usually believe that everyone else has been killed in a barrage and are surprised when everyone (or almost everyone) climbs up out of his hole when it is over.

• Train how to dig in to protect against bombardment. Dig in at every location (balancing the amount of digging against other missions, enemy, terrain, troops, and time available factors). Take pride in camouflage, dispersion, and light discipline.

(2) Train soldiers in active defensive tactics.

• Drill troops in how to defeat infantry and armor forces.

• Drill troops in air defense tactics. Train all who are not in the direct path of an attacking aircraft to engage it with their rifles. This is as much a protective measure against battle fatigue as it is an air defense technique since it changes them from being helpless victims to being hunters who are helping their buddies.

NOTE: Being hit by friendly fire (whether direct or indirect) or losing troops in a senseless accident produces more battle fatigue because one cannot strike back and it seems so needless.

(3) Drill to prevent friendly fire casualties.

• Drill relentlessly in identification of combat vehicles, equipment, and aircraft to minimize mistakes in identification.

• Remind everyone that our weapons and those of our allies and potential adversaries have been sold around the world and could end up on either or both sides in any conflict. Know the weapons the enemy is using. Drill to identify enemy weapons and weapons systems by name.

　　• Practice rigorous coordination and communication within and between units.

　　　• Ensure all personnel are proficient in and knowledgeable of the procedures for challenging, identifying, and communicating with US and allied ground and air forces. Practice these procedures frequently during all operational and environmental conditions to identify and correct any deficiencies.

　　　• Inform everyone, down to the lowest level, of the friendly forces likely to be encountered in the scheme of maneuver, but be alert and ready for the possibility of change without notice, including the enemy appearing where friends are expected and vice versa.

　　　• Continually conduct risk assessment and control procedures.

　　(4) Frequently review the TSOP for rules of engagement, danger, and close fire support, and modify or change as required. Maintain the best balance between suppressing or destroying the enemy's capability to inflict damage on us while preventing mistaken fire on friendly forces.

A-6. IMMOBILITY

　　a.　*Risk Factor:* Immobility during static, heavy fighting.

　　　• The highest rates of battle fatigue have usually been in static situations where the fighting is heavy, resulting in little opportunity to move around. This occurs when troops are pinned down in bunkers, trenches, or ruins (WWI and Korean War trench lines, Anzio in WWII). It occurs for the attacker and the defender who must fight at close quarters, day after day, and for armored troops when they are deployed on restrictive terrain.

　　　• Conversely, during highly mobile warfare, whether maneuvering in battle, pursuing, or even in hasty retreat, obvious battle fatigue symptoms and casualties often are not recognized until a safe place or stable lull is reached. (However, many soldiers may have been killed, wounded, or missing as a direct consequence of battle fatigue symptoms but were not classified as battle fatigue casualties.)

b. *Leader Actions:* Recognize the static, heavy fighting and institute protective measures for trench, bunker, or urban warfare.

• Rotate units frequently back to reserve positions where they can move around freely whenever the tactical situation permits.

• Keep the troops informed and try to give them the best possible support for food, water, clothing, supplies, and mail up to the farthest forward positions.

A-7. LACK OF INFORMATION/SUPPORT

a. *Risk Factor:* Lack of information and failure of expected support. When troops do not know what is planned, they feel isolated, unappreciated, and forgotten. Whenever support or relief does not show up, they may feel deserted. This is especially true if the failure is unexplained. They lose the perspective of the greater mission and are less able to maintain a positive perspective on the combat stressors. They tend to fear the worst, and rumors take hold and lead to battle fatigue and even panic.

b. *Leader Actions:* Keep information flowing.

(1) Keep yourself informed.

• Actively seek out information from the chain of command, the chain of support, and other reliable sources.

• Do not ignore less reliable sources of information, but try to get confirmation before committing totally to act on it.

(2) Keep all the troops informed with the best, honest information.

• Keep the troops well-informed of their goals, the situation, and how they are doing. Information flow must be a routine, ongoing process which is transmitted down to the lowest level. Explain to troops that information will be disseminated through the chain of command.

• Use in-country public affairs assets. Public affairs can play a key role in helping commanders meet the communications needs of their soldiers. Public affairs officers advise commanders and their leaders on the information needs of units, assisting in the development of messages, facilitating the flow of information, and providing communications channels.

• Stop rumors and counsel rumor-mongers while giving out the best, most reliable information you have, with appropriate caveats about its limitations. Remember, even telling the troops that you do not have any new information is meaningful information to them. It lets them know that you are keeping them informed.

• Tell the troops what kind of supporting arms are expected, but explain that other units and missions also have a claim to them and support may not be immediate.

• Do not conceal unpleasant possibilities, but put dangers in the perspective of how the unit will prepare to overcome them. Always give them some guidance they can begin to act on and not just sit and worry.

• When operational security does not permit informing the troops on upcoming operations, keep them informed in other areas. Once the security requirements are lifted, brief the troops and provide as much information as possible.

A-8. NUCLEAR, BIOLOGICAL, AND CHEMICAL WEAPONS

a. *Risk Factor:* High threat of NBC weapons use and actual use. The invisible, pervasive nature of many of these weapons creates a high degree of uncertainty and ambiguity with fertile opportunity for false alarms, rumors, and maladaptive stress reactions. The terrible nature of some of these weapons will create fear for the future, the homeland, and perhaps even for the survival of civilization.

b. *Leader Actions:* Prepare troops for NBC threat contingencies.

(1) Keep information flowing, dispel myths, and control rumors.

• Discuss the situation and its possible long-term implications honestly.

• Maintain the view that the best chance for the future will be maintained if the unit stays effective.

(2) In training, emphasize that our intention is deterrence.

• Tell the lesson of history that NBC weapons are much less likely to be used against us if we show by our defensive training that they will not give an enemy enough advantage to justify the risk of his using them against us. If we train and the enemy does use them, we also have our best chance of surviving and winning.

(3) Put NBC (and especially chemical) defense in realistic perspective.

• Point out that low-dose exposure will be much more common than high-dose (potentially lethal) exposure.

• Compare the risks of the most likely threat with the increased risk of facing the conventional threat in varying levels of MOPP. Think of the decision to put yourself or your unit into MOPP as being like the decision of how much cover to take when under the threat of conventional weapons when you have a mission to accomplish.

• Change to MOPP levels that permit accomplishment of the mission and survival of the soldier.

(4) Practice flexible MOPP procedures when there is only a threat of chemical agent use, or low doses in the surrounding areas, and there is a critical mission to be done that is impaired or endangered by MOPP.

• Mission-oriented protective posture flexibility means that some team members perform the mission-essential heavy work, fine finger movements, and visual and auditory tasks at a lower level of MOPP (or mask only) while others stay at a higher MOPP level.

• Those in high MOPP stay ready to take over the task and provide assistance to the members of the first group as they go to MOPP Level 4 if the unit is hit with chemicals.

• In any potential biological or chemical risk situation, some members of the unit are at some protective level at all times, with MOPP rotation set by the TSOP.

(5) Emphasize buddy aid by those in MOPP rather than self-administration of antidotes such as atropine, which may have harmful effects if taken in the absence of nerve agents.

• Soldiers may take the first autoinjection of atropine (Mark I Kit) if they believe they have been exposed.

• Get to a buddy to confirm the symptoms within 10-15 minutes and administer a second Mark I only if it is truly needed.

(6) Reduce ambiguity by having a unit TSOP with clear, objective criteria for all levels of MOPP.

• Some members of the team automatically mask or go to MOPP Level 1 or 2 whenever any unidentified aircraft are seen, or potentially contaminated patients arrive, or there is incoming artillery or smoke. They monitor the detection equipment and prepare to give aid if agents are present.

• Those who are performing critical jobs which cannot be performed well in mask or overgarment continue to perform those tasks. They stay ready to go to a protective posture immediately if a NBC threat is confirmed.

• Specify in the TSOP how to decrease MOPP levels and unmask sequentially as a team, not all at once. The unmasking drill needs to be practiced. Give active reassurance to the first group to unmask, assuring them that their buddies are observing and can help them if any harmful agent is present.

(7) Train in the protective mask often and require prolonged wear. It takes repeated familiarization and time to acclimate and get over the common claustrophobic feeling. The respiratory threat from almost all NBC agents is much greater than the skin contact threat. Inhaled nerve or cyanide kills in minutes. Inhaled blister and choking agents act slowly, but once they are in the lungs, one cannot get them out. Absorption of most agents through the skin is slower. This allows time to wash them off and use antidotes if available.

• Start with enjoyable activities to overcome initial anxiety.

• Wear the mask often in garrison, even at desk jobs. The more often soldiers wear their mask the quicker they become familiar with it.

• Have periodic prolonged wear (8+ hours) to help soldiers realize they can tolerate the discomfort of the mask.

• Wear the mask while performing tasks which relate to combat duties.

• Wear the gloves often (with and without mask) until most of the essential jobs can be done in them.

(8) Train sometimes in MOPP Level 4 (or simulated MOPP Level 4, which is to overdress while wearing the protective mask, overboots, and gloves). However, this training is less important than mastering the mask alone.

(9) Issue each soldier his own personal mask whenever feasible. This ensures that each soldier's mask is the correct size and places responsibility for care of the mask on each soldier. A soldier

will feel more trust, confidence, and even grudging "cohesion" for his mask if it is his and he is issued the same mask every time.

(10) Use any mask confidence exercise only as a culmination of training and proof of success. This requires teams to enter an area where a riot control agent has been released and—

• Perform their team jobs together.

• Drink water through the drinking tube.

• Unmask briefly while holding their breath and keeping their eyes closed.

• Remask, reseal, and clear the mask before breathing. The soldier can then leave without feeling unpleasant symptoms from the tear gas if everything works well. The purpose of the exercise is to build confidence in the mask, not to destroy it.

(11) Emphasize professionalism in training.

• Conduct cross-training to allow effective crew rotation and physical conditioning which extends the limits of the soldier.

• Emphasize the common soldiering skills.

• Emphasize that we train to do our missions this way because it is the TSOP. We do it because we are smart, survival-skilled soldiers.

• Practice all critical tasks with at least the mask on until they can be done automatically. This is essential.

Simple routine or overlearned tasks are the least susceptible to degradation.

(12) Leaders must be positive role models. They must be highly visible and positive in doing the MOPP training themselves.

(13) Make NBC field training exercises realistic.

• Integrate NBC conditions into realistic training exercises. Cohesion and esprit de corps are achieved by working together to overcome (or prevail in spite of) hardship and discomfort which NBC training provides.

• Work together as a team to develop coping techniques which deal with individual limitations encountered while performing routine tasks during realistic training.

• Develop and practice ways to identify individuals in MOPP, to assess their alertness, comprehension, and well-being, and to give and receive emotional support.

• Make frequent use of simulated agents such as methyl salicylate (oil of wintergreen). These provide realistic practice with detection equipment and protective gear.

• Teach threat limitations as well as strengths. For example, teach that the threat is not everywhere but decreases with distance from point of dispersal and time and can be reduced by skilled use of terrain, cover, and wind direction.

• Stress the need for contamination avoidance and use of collective protection and decontamination means. Also stress individual, crew, and unit proficiency in the tactics, techniques, and procedures of NBC defense.

• Make exercise scenarios plausible. Exercise detection, monitoring, reporting, and risk estimation.

• Use reports of nuclear weapons explosions only if they fit well in the exercise scenario. Since we cannot adequately simulate a real nuclear burst, use "precautionary alerts" to exercise TSOP.

• Make the dispersal and "hardening" of a unit's position the unit's standard way of setting up (so that it is less vulnerable to nuclear flash and blast). Reinforce this by frequent practice and nuclear blast and radiation protective drills, both for what to do with a few minutes advance warning and for when the first warning is just the flash.

(14) Train hard and be prepared to manage heat stress in well-acclimatized, fit soldiers. We must push our well-prepared troops to a level of acceptable risk.

• Be alert and fully prepared to manage heat stress (heat cramps, heat exhaustion, and even the exceedingly early signs of heat stroke [which are revealed by mental symptoms of elation, confusion, disorientation, and perhaps hallucinations and belligerence before they progress to coma, seizures, and danger of permanent brain damage or death]).

• Take this risk only after specific preparation of every soldier involved and of the unit. Adequate preparation includes—

• Physical (aerobic and muscle) fitness.

Acclimatization to the area of operations and conditioning to various MOPP levels, especially MOPP Levels 3 and 4.

    • Acclimatization by doing more work in hot conditions.

    • Water availability and command emphasis on drinking "by the numbers" (so much per hour).

NOTE: Leaders must be concerned about soldiers' health, but they should be careful not to lose credibility through overreaction to perceived hazards.

    • Skin and foot care.

    • Medical awareness with backup personnel and preparation of evacuation means.

    • Management of psychological stress symptoms, such as hyperventilation, by using self-calming relaxation and buddy aid techniques.

★   ★   ★

WARNING

Unfit, unacclimatized troops should not be overexerted in training as this could cause severe injury or even death. A special physical training program will be required to integrate such soldiers into a regular Army physical training program.

★   ★   ★

    (15) Emphasize the importance of timely prophylactic/treatment materials once the causative chemical or biological agent is known.

A-9. DEPRIVED OF SLEEP

    a. *Risk Factor:* Sleep loss. Battle fatigue can occur without sleep loss, but insufficient sleep can be a major contributing factor. The sleep-deprived soldier or leader has difficulty thinking and reasoning and becomes easily confused and overly suggestible with poor judg-

ment. Pessimistic thinking takes hold and everything seems too difficult. Sleep loss alone can cause the tired brain to see things which are
not there (visual hallucinations) or to perceive things which are there
as something totally different. When anxiety and vigilance (staying
awake on watch) are added, the soldier may be temporarily unable to
distinguish between reality and what he fears. Normal physical symptoms of stress can become magnified into disabling illnesses.

b. *Leader Actions:* Practice sleep discipline and sleep planning.
Sleep discipline means sleeping when and where you are directed.
Sleep discipline is intended to provide the best sleep possible in the
time and place available. Because battle is both stressful and unpredictable, a flexible plan is needed to supply everyone with sufficient
sleep.

(1) Set shifts whenever possible.

• Shifts which allow each individual 6 to 8 hours of continuous sleep when feasible are preferred. Provide soldiers with a minimum of 4 hours of uninterrupted sleep in a 24 hour period (6-8 hours
optimum). This greatly extends soldiers and crew endurance limits.

• The standard wartime shift is 12 hours on and 12 hours off
(two shifts per day). This has the advantage of simplicity, requires
fewer skilled personnel, and has only two shift changes when information must be exchanged.

(2) Supervisors should consider alternative shift plans, if flexibility of sleep hours is required in a combat mission situation. For
many jobs, 12 hours on duty may be too mentally or physically exhausting, leading to poor performance in the last several hours. Or the
work load may be so variable that it is sometimes necessary to keep
both shifts on duty, in which case one shift may have to go 36 hours
without sleep.

• The sleep does not have to be continuous. While 6 to 8 hours
of continuous sleep is preferred, studies show that several blocks of
sleep which add up to 6 hours in 24 are adequate for most people. The
fewer the blocks, the better.

• Consider two shifts per day, each working 6 hours on, 6
hours off, (or 6½ on, 5½ off, with overlap for shift changes). This works
everyone half the time, but gives everyone two chances each day to get

3 to 5 hours of sleep. The world's sailing navies used 4 hours on, 4 hours off for centuries because of the heavy work and frequent need to call all hands on deck.

• Use the 6 hours on, 6 hours off alternative only in work situations where the duty station, dining facility, sleeping quarters, and other essentials are close together, such as in small base areas. Otherwise, too much time is wasted going back and forth to quarters and the dining facility.

• Ensure all essential information is transmitted and understood when the shifts change.

• Avoid shifts which set the period of sleep at different times each day—such as 8 hours on, 8 hours off. This tends to disrupt the body's 24 hour/day biological rhythm and leads to poor performance as well as personal discomfort. Whenever possible, people should get at least some sleep at the same time each day.

NOTE: In CONOPS, if shifts are impractical, try to give all individuals at least 4 hours of uninterrupted sleep each 24 hours (5 hours if sleep is interrupted).

(3) Identify and take special precautions to protect the performance of those critical tasks which are vulnerable (sensitive and likely to break down) due to sleep loss, especially planning, initiating, reasoning, cognition, and vigilance. Remember, 4 hours each 24 hours is far from ideal.

• Do not go with only 4 hours sleep each 24 hours for more than 1 or 2 weeks before paying back sleep debt.

• If at all possible, give the individuals whose key tasks are vulnerable to sleep loss 6 hours sleep a day.

(4) Assign naps.

• It is helpful to get 1 hour sleep here, 2 hours there. Even a little sleep is better than none. It is not necessary that it all be in one block.

• Even brief (15 to 30 minute) naps help against sleep debt. However, 5-minute naps do not help.

• Plan time to wake up from naps. After a nap, mental task

performance is often much worse for several minutes after waking up than it was just before the person went to sleep. The brain needs time to "warm up."

(5) Practice counterfatigue measures to use when soldiers must continue to work or fight without enough sleep.

• Use ways to increase alertness.

    • Add changing sensations. Of course, this must not interfere with the task. For example, one can listen to the radio while driving on the highway at night but not on guard duty. It is best for the soldier not to be too comfortable. He can snack on something with a strong taste. Protein is better than carbohydrates for staying alert. Caution is needed in using stimulant drugs. Caffeine (coffee, tea, and cola) is relatively safe for most people for short-term use, but may make it difficult to sleep when opportunities arise. Amphetamines and other strong stimulant drugs are more dangerous; they can cause panic attacks, hyperactivity, and temporary paranoid psychotic reactions which last several days. Also, people "crash" when they stop using such strong stimulants and many even get seriously depressed.

    • Add physical movement if the task lacks it. The soldier should take stretch breaks and jog to increase circulation. He should fidget in place if he cannot leave the duty station.

    • Add social stimulation. Use the buddy system, assigning two people to work together. Of course, this means one fewer person is getting time to sleep. With workers who must be at different isolated locations, alternate having them call each other by radio or telephone to ensure that they remain alert.

    • Add sense of urgency. Brief troops about the urgency of the task. Be sure to explain why it is important to stay awake. If it is hard to keep urgency in mind, use "game playing" to maintain interest by adding competition or suspense.

    • Add feedback of performance. If the task does not automatically provide feedback, actively try to create it. The leader can provide feedback by spot-checking for compliance, building feedback into the task, and contacting the users of the service to make sure they are satisfied.

    • Rotate jobs. If the job requires continual attention or is physically demanding, it will be vulnerable to sleep loss. If you cannot provide breaks, try having people switch jobs, preferably to something quite different. This can give surprising improvement in performance, provided the soldier knows how to do the new job well. In order to rotate jobs, you must have cross-trained personnel in advance. Make sure all essential information is exchanged, understood, and recorded when the switch is being made. Otherwise, worse difficulties may result.

• Use ways to support memory.

• Clarify and modify the task. Try to simplify orders and complex sequences. This has to be done before people get too tired to use good judgment. Double-check such sequences (get independent verification). Document in writing what was done.

• Use performance aids, if new learning is needed. Take notes. Draw simple diagrams or maps to involve visual-spatial memory as well as verbal memory. Write down all orders and read back input to ensure that it has been understood and copied correctly. Refer to these aids later when short-term memory has forgotten exactly what was said.

• Drill the task to "overlearn it" until it is automatic. The common saying is "He knows it so well he can do it in his sleep." Even complex tasks will be resistant to sleep loss if they have been practiced until they need only be started to run themselves through to completion without having to think about them.

• Build in cues and reminders of the self-initiated parts within the tasks itself or the situation. Have checklists and TSOP, put up signs, write notes—then practice! This is especially relevant for tasks, such as preventive maintenance and ordering more supplies. These are easily omitted by tired workers, but the whole mission may collapse suddenly if they are not done.

• Determine performance decrement factors through realistic mission training in MOPP Levels 3 and 4. These factors can then be used to state realistic mission requirements for units and crews.

• Divide the labor (task paralleling). Put more people to doing the entire job. This works if having more people doing the same overall task means less work for each person and especially if it gives more time for each element of the task. Of course, it also means that fewer people are getting to sleep, and it is harder to coordinate the information, so do this only for essential, critical tasks. Let the other tasks wait (see priorities, below).

• Divide the responsibilities of the time-shared task where one person normally has to do two or three things all mixed together. Assign several people, but modify the task so that each person has responsibility for only one task element and can concentrate fully on it. The hidden danger of this remedy shows up if several people mst transmit information among themselves, since communication and memory are impaired by sleep loss.

• Simplify priorities. Sleep-deprived people have trouble deciding what is most important. They tend to hang up on choices (taking longer and longer, or not choosing at all), or they unthinkingly do what is easiest, or most learned, or most obvious. Specify what is most important versus what should be dropped out. You should decide this while fresh, build it into your TSOP, and practice it.

(6) Get good sleep before CONOPS or an afternoon nap before night operations. You cannot "stockpile" sleep, but starting out without any sleep debt delays the onset of degraded performance.

• In CONOPS or SUSOPS, never waste a chance to let someone in the unit sleep. Spread such opportunities around to give everyone enough.

NOTE: Be careful. Do not allow sleep in unsafe conditions, such as under vehicles or in vehicles with the motors running. Beware of the tendency for tired people to slack off and use poor judgment.

A-10. PHYSICALLY RUN-DOWN

a. *Risk Factor:* Run-down physical condition. This contributes to battle fatigue by sapping soldiers' ability to function and, therefore, their confidence to accomplish the mission and survive. Neither physical fatigue nor sleep loss necessarily causes battle fatigue, but they can be strong contributing factors. To the extent that these factors are involved, they are easier to prevent or correct than are most of the factors listed earlier. The more physical exhaustion is present in battle

fatigue casualties, the more confident we can be that soldiers will recover completely. These soldiers return to duty once we have replen-
ished the physical resources. However, our treatment must also
restore their confidence.

(1) Dehydration deserves special mention because it can be
extremely subtle.

• A stressed soldier under battlefield MOPP, or heavy work
conditions can become exceedingly dehydrated without feeling
thirsty. This is especially true in hot climates, in MOPP, or the
arctic. Dehydration renders the blood less able to carry oxygen to the
brain and muscles. This results in instant battle fatigue.

• Colonel (later Brigadier General) S.L.A. Marshall, the US
Army historian who pioneered the technique of interviewing combat
teams while the battle was still going on, discovered this in himself
during his first exploratory mission on Kwajalein in WWII. Colonel
Marshall was a man who was literally fearless, so this came as a surprise to him. He summarized the lesson by writing, "No one ever told
me that dehydration causes cowardice in its most abject form."

2) Poor diet is common, if not inevitable, in combat and tends
to lower one's energy level and sense of being strong and alert. While
some people eat more when anxious or depressed, most eat less.
Stomach pain and nausea are common signs of battle fatigue which
further inhibit eating. The monotony and unpalatability of some
meal(s), ready to eat (MRE) or tray-packs (T Rations), will not help.
Such rations are even less likely to be eaten if they must be eaten cold.
Many soldiers may start eating only a few, select items which do not
provide all-around nutrition.

(3) Poor hygiene is common, if not inevitable, in combat and
tends to lower one's energy level and sense of being alert and
"human." We have all had the experience of coming in from days out
in the field, dragging, and how much better we felt after that first hot
shower. Imagine how much worse the "dragging" is if that poor hygiene goes on for weeks. Poor hygiene can also lead to disease.

(4) Low-grade environmental or stress-related illnesses further sap the soldiers' strength and confidence. Chronic diarrhea,
persistent cramps in the stomach, fever from malaria or virus, or skin

infections or blisters that do not heal can make soldiers feel exhausted and demoralized, setting them up for battle fatigue. Units whose leaders do not monitor and enforce basic preventive medicine and hygiene measures are likely to suffer low morale and high battle fatigue rates. Conversely, being in a unit where a sense of caring, order, and TSOP is maintained is a strong stress reducer. It not only maintains health but also promotes unit pride, cohesion, and confidence.

b. *Leader Actions:* Protect the physical well-being of the troops. In combat, never waste the strength of the soldiers for trivial matters because there will be many occasions when it will be necessary for soldiers to accept hardship to gain the advantage.

(1) Ensure the best water, food, equipment, shelter, and sanitation (and sleep) possible under the circumstances of the mission.

• Enforce water discipline.

• Enforce food discipline; ensure soldiers eat an adequate balanced diet from their MRE, T Rations, or A Rations.

• Enforce basic personal hygiene and preventive medicine practices.

• Assure latrines are kept clean.

• Provide time for troops to bath or shower at least once weekly and more often when feasible.

(2) Explain why the hardship is necessary when unable to provide well for the soldiers' physical needs.

• Put it back in the perspective of how "we will cope."

• Remind them of those times in earlier training when they overcame the hardship to accomplish the mission.

A-11. INADEQUATE FITNESS

a. *Risk Factor:* Lack of physical fitness. Being physically fit is not a guarantee against becoming a battle fatigue casualty, but not being physically fit is an invitation for it. Sudden overuse of the cardiovascular system, muscles, joints, and bones that have not been prepared for the strain can lead to immediate failure and serious injury. Even if these are avoided, the unfit soldiers will be subject to days of stiffness, aching, and weakness. During this time, they are at extremely high risk for battle fatigue, especially if further demands are made on them.

b. *Leader Actions:* Assure physical fitness.

• Physical fitness programs are useful in promoting unit cohesion, but they are also important in themselves as protection against battle fatigue. Being super-fit is not a guarantee against disabling battle fatigue, but it does increase self-confidence (and the confidence of buddies) and delays the onset of muscular fatigue.

• Assure that everyone in the unit has—

• Aerobic fitness (endurance).

• The necessary muscle strength in the parts of the body which they will use in their combat role.

• Calluses in the right places (to avoid developing blisters).

• The necessary flexibility and agility for the tasks to be done, including the combat self-defense tasks like digging. This is especially necessary for some combat support/CSS personnel whose garrison or field jobs tend to be sedentary

A-12. OLDER VETERAN OR SHORT-TIMER

a. *Risk Factor:* Cumulative combat exposure or "being short."

• These are special situations where the individual is at high risk for battle fatigue.

• The "old sergeant syndrome" of WWII occurred in the veteran soldier who had been in combat for a long time. He had risen to a responsible position but had seen all his old buddies killed or wounded and replaced by new, inexperienced soldiers. The only way home was death, mutilation, or, if exceedingly lucky, the "million dollar wound." Although he often insisted that he wanted to stay in combat, he felt guilt at his weakness. He had become overly cautious, indecisive, anxious, and depressed.

• An "old sergeant" variation, seen also in Vietnam, was the NCO or officer who extended for a second or third tour but who was so embittered and hardened to combat that he was in danger of committing some of the misconduct stress behaviors.

• "Short" soldiers are those who are coming close to the date when they will rotate home from the combat tour. Neither they nor their buddies want them to get hit on their last day (or week, or month, or mission) in combat. This was a common experience in Vietnam (with the 365-day tour) and in Korea (with the "point system" used late in the war). In WWII, it was seen in aircrews who rotated home after some number of missions, and in the Marines when it was established that they would be rotated home after three amphibious operations. A similar reaction may occur in the last days before an expected cease-fire or armistice.

  b. *Leader Actions:* Recognize and manage the "old veteran" or "short-timer" syndrome.

    • Maintain a rotation schedule which avoids relieving soldiers from dangerous duty prematurely at the expense of others, without keeping them in so long that they become ineffective and dangerous.

    • Develop rotation standards based on the overall situation.

    • Reassign the "old veteran" to a responsible rear echelon job rather than risk a serious failure in combat or a case of battle fatigue that does not respond to treatment and leaves the soldier permanently scarred.

    • Support and protect those individuals who are showing more signs of battle fatigue than the average. This is done without creating a social expectation of relief from dangerous duty that saps the fighting strength.

    • Use judgment when discussing this topic so that it does not become a "self-fulfilling prophecy."

    • Do not set an automatic policy of relieving "short" soldiers from dangerous missions during their final weeks. This will move the "short-timer" syndrome even earlier in the last months.

    • Give the individual soldiers (or units) who are preparing to rotate home a period of several days of minimal danger just before departure.

    • Schedule this time for postdeployment debriefings. These sessions are similar to the routine after-action debriefings but on a larger scale.

    • Concentrate on remembering and reviewing in detail the major events (good and bad) of the tour, sharing the common experiences and feelings.

    • Actively work through unresolved, painful, or controversial issues.

• Discuss (receive briefings on) how the home front (family, Army, nation) may have changed or may react to returning veterans and their needs.

• Normalize the common postcombat (traumatic) stress signs/symptoms most will have.

• Review coping techniques.

• Conduct a suitable memorial ceremony prior to departure from the combat zone to provide a sense of completion and closure for those soldiers returning home.

• Coordinate with the rear detachment and family support group to schedule information briefings pertaining to redeployment of the unit to its home station.

• Plan a welcome home/memorial ceremony which includes the family and garrison community.

ORGANIZATION AND FUNCTIONS OF ARMY MEDICAL DEPARTMENT COMBAT STRESS CONTROL UNITS

B-1. INTRODUCTION

Combat stress control is now recognized as an Army Medical Department functional area for doctrinal and planning purposes. As such, it is distinguished from the other nine Army Medical Department functional areas of health service support which are—

    a.   Patient evacuation and medical regulating.

    b.   Hospitalization.

    c.   Health service logistics/blood management.

    d.   Dental services.

    e.   Veterinary services.

    f.   Preventive medicine services.

    g.   Area medical support.

    h.   Command, control, communications, computers, and intelligence (C4I).

    i.   Medical laboratory services.

B-2. ARMY MEDICAL DEPARTMENT COMBAT STRESS CONTROL PROGRAM

    a.   Combat stress control refers to a coordinated program for the prevention and treatment of battle fatigue and other harmful stress-related behaviors. Combat stress control is implemented by mental health personnel organic to units and by specialized medical combat stress control units which are a corps-level (or echelon above corps) asset. The combat stress control organization must function flexibly across the full range of combat intensities and operational scenarios including war and operations other than war.

b.　There are six major combat stress control programs or functions which have different relative importance in different scenarios. The usual order of priority is as follows:

(1) *Consultation.* Liaison, preventive advice, education programs, planning, and stress control interventions to supported unit commanders and staff.

(2) *Reorganization (reconstitution) support.* Assistance at field locations to battle fatigue units which are withdrawn for rest, reorganization, and integration of new replacements.

(3) *Proximate neuropsychiatric triage.* Sorting battle fatigue cases based on where they can be treated to maximize return to duty, separating out true neuropsychiatric or medical/surgical patients.

(4) *Stabilization.* Immediate, short-term management and evaluation of severely disturbed battle fatigue casualties, neuropsychiatric, and alcohol and drug misuse cases to determine return to duty potential or to permit safe evacuation.

(5) *Restoration.* One to three days of rest, replenishment, and activities to restore confidence of battle fatigue casualties at "forward" medical units.

(6) *Reconditioning.* An intensive 4- to 21-day program of replenishment, physical activity, therapy, and military retraining for battle fatigue casualties and neuropsychiatric cases (including alcohol and drug misuse) who require this to return to duty.

B-3. BASIC TENETS OF ARMY MEDICAL DEPARTMENT COMBAT STRESS CONTROL

a.　Army Medical Department combat stress control is unit-identified and mission-oriented.

(1) The combat stress control concept differs from conventional clinic or community mental health in its explicit identification with and utilization of the strengths of Army organization and ethics.

(2) Mental health personnel assigned combat stress control

duties are clearly identified as members of a specific Army TOE unit. They may be organic members of line medical units (such as the mental health section of the division's medical support company or the corps' area support medical battalion), or they may be members of a medical combat stress control unit which has a formal support relationship with the line units (such as a medical detachment or medical company, combat stress control).

(3) Combat stress control personnel work closely with the chain of command and the chain of support in the context of the supported units' changing missions. They work in the supported units' locations, or as close as is feasible under the tactical conditions.

(4) Mental health/combat stress control personnel also work with the individual soldier and (in peacetime) with the soldier's family members. However, these soldiers and families are considered valued members of the supported unit; they are not labeled as patients or clients. Combat stress control personnel begin with a presumption of normality (that the soldier [or family member] is a normal, well-intentioned human being). They presume that these soldiers or family members are trying in good faith to master the sometimes excessive stressors of military life and that they want to succeed. This presumption can only be displaced by a thorough evaluation which proves the contrary, or by failure to improve after sufficient expert treatment.

b.   Army Medical Department combat stress control is proactive and prevention-oriented.

(1) Combat stress control personnel/units dedicate much of their time and resources to activities which assist the commanders of units in controlling stressors. They identify stress problems before they lead to dysfunction or stress casualties. This early identification permits the retention and recovery of mildly and moderately overstressed soldiers, in their units, on duty status.

(2) Even when providing reactive treatment to heavily overstressed soldiers who are in crisis, combat stress control personnel continually look for the primary causal factors (stressors). They work with the chain of command and the chain of support to gain control of the stressors or control stress which may adversely affect soldiers and their families. The objective is not only to help the afflicted sol-

diers and return them to effective duty, but also to prevent future affliction in others.

(3) Even when overcommitted to treating mass casualties, combat stress control units remain alert and prepared to reallocate resources. When necessary, combat stress control resources deploy to support units in forward areas. There, they provide early preventive intervention for stressed soldiers and assist command to gain control of the correctable stressors. The intent of early preventive intervention is to—

• Minimize the flow of battle fatigue casualties.

• Provide treatment for and return to duty of soldiers.

• Minimize the risk of future suffering and disability (prevent PTSD).

B-4. ORGANIZATIONAL AND OPERATIONAL CONCEPT FOR ARMY MEDICAL DEPARTMENT COMBAT STRESS CONTROL

a. *Organic Mental Health Sections.* Mental health personnel are organic to medical elements of divisions, separate brigades, and the area support medical battalion.

(1) Division mental health sections have a psychiatrist, a social work officer, a clinical psychologist, and seven behavioral science specialists. At least one behavioral science NCO and one mental health officer should be allocated routinely to work in each maneuver brigade.

(2) The area support medical battalion has a psychiatrist, a social work officer, and eight behavioral science specialists. A behavioral science NCO may be allocated to work with each area support medical company.

(3) Separate heavy brigade medical companies will have three behavioral science specialists (currently no officer). Some SOF units have a clinical psychologist. Armored cavalry regiments currently have no organic mental health personnel.

b. *Mission of the Organic Mental Health Section.* The mission of the organic mental personnel is to provide command consultation, training, technical supervision, staff planning, and clinical evaluation (neuropsychiatric triage). They must be mobile—able to travel to military units. They can provide brief forward treatment to small numbers of cases during combat operations. Their assets are not sufficient to provide longer treatment for large numbers of battle fatigue or neuropsychiatric casualties without sacrificing their other critical preventive and staff functions.

    c.   *Combat Stress Control on Today's Battlefield.* On today's battlefield, each maneuver brigade covers a larger and more fluid area and has greater fire power and responsibility than did a WWII division. The Army operations concept makes the brigades even more the basic war-fighting echelon. Winning the first battles will be critical and may require reconstitution of attrited units and rapid return of temporarily disabled soldiers to their units. The organic division mental health personnel must be reinforced if cases are to be restored in the brigade and division support areas. Separate brigades and armored cavalry regiments will also require this reinforcement.

    (1) The combat stress control organization must achieve a balance between pre-positioning elements far forward and having other elements further to the rear. The far forward teams provide consultation, triage, and immediate treatment. The rearward teams support rear battle; these teams take the overflow and problem cases from forward areas. The rearward teams are ready on short notice to redeploy forward to the areas of greatest need, such as to the mass casualty or reconstitution sites.

    (2) The organic mental health sections are essential to provide the infrastructure of mental health personnel who share familiarity and trust with unit leaders. These factors are necessary for effective consultation and prevention.

    (3) Under the combat stress control concept, the organic mental health section provides the points of contact for reinforcing elements from corps-level combat stress control units. These higher-echelon elements will deploy into the brigade, division, or corps area to assume the treatment role and assist in other functions. The point of contact is essential for coordinating, updating, orienting, and facilitating the attachment of reinforcing combat stress control elements. A combat stress control team which tries to join a unit during deployment, combat, or reconstitution will be less effective unless

it has mental health points of contact. The mental health points of contact who have developed trust and familiarity with the supported units are of great assistance in facilitating the combat stress control support process.

d.   *Reinforcing Combat Stress Control Teams.* The reinforcing combat stress control teams are small, mobile teams made up of various combinations of the five mental health disciplines. These teams may include a psychiatrist, social work officer, clinical psychologist, psychiatric nurse, occupational therapist, and their enlisted specialists. These teams will have their own tactical vehicles and bring a limited amount of supplies. These combat stress control teams will come from either the medical companies or medical detachments, combat stress control.

(1) The organizational concept for combat stress control packages the five sub-disciplines (officers and enlisted specialists) of the mental health team into 4- or 11-person standard "modular teams." All combat stress control members have basic skills to direct the management of generalized stress casualties while each brings expertise to an area of specific responsibility, to be partially cross-trained to others. Teams are combined into larger task-organized combat stress control elements. The 4- or 11-person teams can be subdivided. Personnel may be cross-attached between teams by their parent combat stress control unit to fit the specific mission. The modified teams and task-organized combat stress control elements will be tailored to make best use of available resources and the abilities and experience of the individual team members.

(2) The combat stress control modular "teams" are as follows:

• Combat stress control preventive teams: Psychiatrist, social work officer, and two behavioral science specialists. The team is allocated one truck with trailer.

• Combat stress control restoration team: Psychiatric nurse, clinical psychologist, occupational therapy officer, two each of their enlisted specialists, noncommissioned officer in charge (NCOIC), and a patient administration specialist. This team is allocated two or three trucks with trailers.

(3) The combat stress control preventive and combat stress control restoration teams are incorporated into two units: medical detachment and medical company, combat stress control.

e. *Medical Detachment, Combat Stress Control*

(1) One combat stress control detachment normally supports one division or two or three separate brigades or regiments.

(2) Each combat stress control detachment has three combat stress control preventive teams and one combat stress control restoration team.

(3) The detachment normally sends combat stress control preventive teams forward to the brigade support areas while the combat stress control restoration team staffs a "fatigue center" for restoration in the division support area or forward corps. While in these areas, the detachment is under operational control of the supported unit. Parts of teams may go forward to ambulance exchange points or maneuver battalions not in contact.

f. *Medical Company, Combat Stress Control*

(1) Each combat stress control company supports two or more divisions in the corps area. Each combat stress control company has six combat stress control preventive teams. These are normally task-organized into two or more elements, ideally one task-organized combat stress control element for each division supported. When total work load allows, each task-organized element staffs a combat fitness reconditioning center, collocated with a corps hospital; this may be augmented with elements of a medical company, holding.

(2) Each task-organized element sends teams to provide consultation to corps units and to reinforce area support medical companies when needed. It maintains contact with the supported division mental health section and combat stress control detachment in the divisions. The combat stress control company sends teams forward to reinforce combat stress control elements as required.

(3) The combat stress control company headquarters collocates with either a medical brigade, medical group, or area support medical battalion headquarters. Combat stress control company support personnel are detailed to the task-organized combat stress control

elements. The combat stress control company exercises command and control for its task-organized combat stress control elements and for the combat stress control detachments which they support.

(4) The combat stress control company reports to and coordinates with the mental health staff sections of the medical group and medical brigade. These small headquarters staff sections advise and assist the combat stress control company regarding the employment, support, and reallocation of combat stress control assets to support the corps' area of operations.

g. *Combat Stress Control in Army Operations.*

(1) The combat stress control organization is designed to be utilized for war and operations other than war. In war, their primary mission is prevention and rapid return to duty of battle fatigue casualties. Teams must be available in sufficient numbers, pre-positioned forward to react immediately, with rearward teams ready to reinforce forward where battle fatigue casualties occur.

(2) In operations other than war, fewer combat stress control units are needed. These combat stress control units are dispersed in support of division mental health and corps units. The focus of their support is the prevention of misconduct stress behaviors and perhaps treatment of substance misuse in theater.

(3) Prevention of PTSD by predeployment briefings, after-action debriefings, and prehomecoming debriefings is a concern at all intensities.

(4) In peacetime, combat stress control detachments (both Active Component and Reserve Component) must habitually train with the divisions they supported during wartime (and/or with other similar divisions). The combat stress control company must develop similar habitual relationships with units in their corps and with the corps' combat stress control detachments. Combat stress control teams should routinely augment organic mental health sections. They should work with maneuver brigades/regiments which lack organic mental health to provide preventive consultation and practice their combat role.

B-5. COMBAT STRESS CONTROL IN THE CONTINUUM OF ARMY LIFE

Combat stress control is not simply a medical responsibility. Fundamentally, it is a leadership responsibility at all echelons. Since stress can have a monumental impact (positive or negative) on the military, stress control activities should be a part of many Army activities. The stress control effort must be concentrated in all three continuums of Army life which are—

- Responsibility.
- Location.
- Mission.

A weakness or a gap at any point defined by those three continuums can cause weakness, overload, or breakdown at points along the other continuums. All players along the dimensions of responsibility, especially the mental health/combat stress control personnel, need to achieve and maintain the broad, three-dimensional system perspective.

UNITED STATES ARMY BANDS

C-1. MORALE SUPPORT

Morale support is essential to the maintenance of our soldiers' will to fight and win. Morale and esprit can be seriously undermined by the stress of battle, and they are the primary targets of enemy psychological warfare. Consequently, they demand the continuing attention of commanders at all levels.

C-2. ARMY BANDS AS EFFECTIVE TOOLS

To meet these challenges, the commander needs an effective means at his disposal that stimulates positive internal and external support for the Army's objectives. Army bands are particularly effective tools at the commander's disposal in building, reinforcing, and maintaining good morale and esprit, as well as countering enemy psychological operations (PSYOP).

C-3. ARMY BANDS IN COMBAT

During the US Army's past wars and conflicts, bands have ranged throughout the battlefield and rear areas performing music. Today's Army bands are CSS units allocated to theater armies, theater Army area commands, corps, divisions, theater defense brigades, selected major Army commands, selected installations, and other selected commands. Army bands provide live music for the troops whenever opportunities present themselves in peace and in war. Army bands are combat-ready units capable of assisting commanders with prescribed missions in the same manner that all CSS units provide support.

C-4. MISSION

The mission of each Army band is specified in paragraph 1, Section 1, of its TOE. This mission may be slightly modified to fit local command needs and exigencies. Army bands promote readiness and relieve stress by enhancing troop morale and unit esprit. They provide music for troop gatherings and activities, military and religious ceremonies, and PSYOP.

C-5. TROOP GATHERINGS AND ACTIVITIES

Army bands provide their most effective dimension of musical support at locations where troops are gathered such as points of embarkation and debarkation, stand-down areas, dispersal areas, hospitals and clearing stations, messing areas, training areas, and rest and recuperation centers. By providing live music for entertainment at such areas, bands help commanders relieve the stress of combat as well as counter loneliness, resignation, alienation, and other threats to the morale and esprit of their soldiers.

C-6. MILITARY CEREMONIES

Army bands provide music for military ceremonies such as reviews, parades, memorial services, and military funerals. This supports the objectives of the unit, building the common spirit that exists between soldiers, raising the soldier above himself, and helping to forge a strong regard for the honor and achievement of the unit by building enthusiasm, motivation, and continued devotion to duty.

C-7. RELIGIOUS CEREMONIES

Army bands enhance worship and religious and memorial ceremonies on the battlefield. This contributes to the strengthening of a soldier's moral values, his commitment to his unit and fellow soldiers, and deepens his respect for the dignity of the individual embodied in his nationhood. Participation in religious ceremonies by an Army band is in accordance with AR 165-1.

C-8. MUSIC IN SUPPORT OF PSYCHOLOGICAL OPERATIONS

    a.   Army bands can contribute significantly to the combat effort when effectively integrated into strategic, operational, and tactical PSYOP. Army bands can reduce the effectiveness of enemy PSYOP directed toward friendly forces and supporting civilian groups.

b.   In meeting his commander's needs for music in combat, the band commander tailors his unit to meet mission requirements. When manned and equipped at current authorized allowances, Army bands are capable of providing marching, concert, and popular (ethnic, cultural, or regional) music performances.

THE UNIT MINISTRY TEAM'S ROLE IN COMBAT STRESS CONTROL AND BATTLE FATIGUE MINISTRY

D-1. INTRODUCTION

This appendix addresses the general role of the unit ministry team in the commander's program of combat stress control and in battle fatigue ministry. The unit ministry team consists of a chaplain and chaplain assistant assigned to units as far forward as the brigade, forward support battalion, each maneuver battalion, and some combat support battalions. This team provides immediate support to leaders in fulfilling their battle fatigue identification and intervention responsibilities. The team also assists in training leaders to recognize battle fatigue symptoms. Unit ministry teams provide training in basic counseling skills for enabling soldiers to talk about their stress.

D-2. EFFECTS OF STRESS

Negative effects of stress can be lessened when the soldier is prepared physically, emotionally, and spiritually prior to combat. The unit ministry teams prepare soldiers to manage combat stress with training before and during deployment. This training helps the soldier to draw upon spiritual strength and share strength and confidence during intensive combat.

D-3. TEAM RELATIONSHIP

The unit ministry team's relationship with the unit promotes trust with the soldiers. Embedding the team in maneuver battalions enables it to respond readily to the needs of soldiers experiencing combat stress and battle fatigue. A person-oriented resource, the team gives religious support to battle fatigue casualties, especially soldiers having less severe difficulties who have rapid replenishment potential.

D-4. SPIRITUAL VALUES

Soldiers' inner resources are often based on their religious and spiritual values. In combat, soldiers show more interest in their religious beliefs. When religious and spiritual values are challenged during the chaos of combat, soldiers may lose sight of inner resources that sustain them. The soldiers then become targets of fear, despair, hopelessness, and eventually, battle fatigue casualties. They are also at risk for committing misconduct stress behaviors. The unit ministry team is the primary resource available to soldiers experiencing these dilemmas and seeking to refocus their spiritual values.

D-5. TEAM SUPPORT

Unit ministry teams provide preventive, immediate, and replenishing spiritual and emotional support and care to soldiers experiencing battle fatigue.

a. *Preventive.* The religious support mission of the unit ministry team assists in preventing battle fatigue and misconduct stress behaviors through establishment of a presence within the unit. It is important for the unit ministry team to be present with soldiers when the unit trains and when it deploys. The unit ministry team can be a calming influence on soldiers; the team can help soldiers strengthen or regain values important to them. Some of the things the unit ministry team does to prevent battle fatigue and misconduct include the following:

   • Being present with the soldiers and deploying with the unit.

   • Providing opportunities for private and group prayer and worship.

   • Providing personal religious articles and materials.

   • Reading the scriptures with soldiers.

   • Providing sacraments as the situation allows.

• Communicating with soldiers, allowing them to work through stress, fear, anxiety, anger, and frustration.

• Visiting soldiers in work and living areas.

• Assisting soldiers and families prior to deployment with preparation for geographical separation and an uncertain future through programs which emphasize family strengths. This helps soldiers to know that their families are cared for during deployment.

b. *Immediate.* The unit ministry team assists commanders in the identification of soldiers experiencing battle fatigue. They work closely with the unit leadership and the medical personnel in battle fatigue care. Chaplains and chaplain assistants are trained to recognize the signs of battle fatigue and provide religious support to soldiers experiencing battle fatigue. The unit ministry team establishes rapport with the soldier and assesses his religious needs. The team then performs or offers the type of religious support designed to provide the most comfort. This includes such things as the following:

• Presence with the soldier.

• Conversation and an opportunity to share fears, hopes, and other feelings.

• Prayers: general prayers, prayers for the individual, or prayers for fallen comrades.

• Rites, sacraments, and ordinances as appropriate.

• Reading from sacred scriptures.

c. *Replenishing.* Following an engagement, the unit may require reconstitution through the addition of new personnel. The unit ministry team will find the surviving soldiers may require a rebuilding of the emotional, psychological, and spiritual strength. During this time, the unit ministry team may require assistance from a chaplain support team (TOE 16500LA/B) or other available rear area unit ministry team assets. The team will maintain its ongoing direct religious support functions which include the following:

• Coordinating the availability of worship services, sacraments, rites, and services/ceremonies honoring the dead.

• Facilitating the integration of personnel replacements.

• Facilitating the grief process through personal counseling and memorial services.

• Reinforcing the soldier's sense of self-worth and hope.

• Structuring opportunities for soldiers to talk about what they have experienced in combat and facilitating integration of the combat experience into their lives.

• Preparing for the next stage of battle.

• Providing personal religious articles and materials.

• Securing or providing denominational religious coverage in the unit or for other units.

• Participating in rebuilding the physical, emotional, and spiritual resources of the unit.

The unit ministry team operates with a soldier-focused approach to religious support. The spiritual dimension the team brings to the soldier's situation is an essential element in the replenishment process. Religious support assists the soldier in achieving emotional and spiritual wholeness.

D-6. REINTEGRATION

Following the end of hostilities, the unit ministry team facilitates reintegration of the individual soldier into family relationships and society at large. Many religious support functions remain the same. Expanded religious support functions may also include the following:

• Providing worship events for the entire unit.

• Providing worship events for varied religious denominations.

• Providing briefings which help soldiers recognize, prepare for, and master the stressors of reunion with family.

• Providing structured events to assist soldiers returning to family and civilian life.

• Providing opportunities for soldiers to experience and understand the forgiving and unchanging love of God.

EXAMPLE LESSON PLAN

LESSON TITLE: IDENTIFY, TREAT, AND PREVENT BATTLE FATIGUE.

COURSE PRESENTED TO: Officers, warrant officers, and NCOs at battalion, company, and platoon level of all divisional and nondivisional, active duty, Reserve, and National Guard units.

PLACE: Classroom or field training site.

REFERENCES:

FM 21-20	Physical Fitness Training
FM 22-9	Soldier Performance in Continuous Operations
FM 22-51	Leaders' Manual for Combat Stress Control
FM 22-100	Military Leadership
FM 100-5	Operations
	Unit Combat Mission Statement
	Unit History

STUDY ASSIGNMENT: As directed by the instructor or commander.

STUDENT UNIFORM AND EQUIPMENT: As directed by the instructor or commander.

TOOLS, EQUIPMENT, AND MATERIALS:

GTA 21-3-4, Battle Fatigue, Normal, Common Signs, What to Do for Self and Buddy.

GTA 21-3-5, Battle Fatigue, "More Serious" Signs: Leader Actions.

GTA 21-3-6, Battle Fatigue, Company Leader Actions and Prevention.

PERSONNEL: One instructor.

INSTRUCTIONAL AIDS: Chalk, chalkboard, eraser, and lectern.

TROOP REQUIREMENTS: None.

TRANSPORTATION REQUIREMENTS: None.

RISK ASSESSMENT LEVEL: As directed by the instructor or commander.

SAFETY REQUIREMENT: As directed by the instructor or commander.

METHOD OF INSTRUCTION: Conference/discussion with examples from real situations.

I. INTRODUCTION

A. Opening Statement. During heavy fighting in past wars, the Army usually had one battle fatigue casualty for every three to five soldiers evacuated with wounds. In the 1982 Lebanon Crisis, one Israeli armor unit had one case of battle fatigue for every one wounded in a desperate night action. Israeli CSS soldiers (for example, truck drivers, ordnance technicians) became stress casualties when they saw what modern weapons do to human bodies, even though they themselves were not under attack. However, in elite units (such as Airborne and Rangers in WWII), less than one battle fatigue casualty for every ten wounded occurred, even in extremely intense or prolonged fighting.

This teaching applies specifically to your units and your missions in any level of combat intensity, whether you are combat arms, combat support, or CSS. History shows that most battle-fatigued soldiers can be restored to duty quickly if they rest close to their units and are treated positively as soldiers, not as weaklings, cowards, or sick patients. This restoration requires planning and coordination. If they are evacuated too far to the rear, many may never recover. In the continuous battlefield of war, even the short-term loss of so many trained, combat-experienced soldiers could be disastrous. The Army initiated this combat stress control training program to ensure that all senior NCOs and company-grade officers know what to do about battle fatigue (how to identify it, how to treat it, and how to prevent it). You, in turn, are responsible for teaching your subordinates what they need to know to control battle fatigue and accomplish the mission.

B. *Objectives*

    1.   Enabling Learning Objectives.

        a.   State the definition of battle fatigue.

        b.   State the normal, common signs and the warning (more serious) signs of battle fatigue.

        c.   List the leaders' treatment of normal, common signs and warning signs of battle fatigue.

        d.   Define mild (duty), moderate (rest), and severe (hold/refer) battle fatigue in terms of where each is sent.

        e.   State the principles of preventing battle fatigue.

    2.   Terminal Learning Objective. Discuss leaders' responsibly for identifying, treating, and preventing battle fatigue as discussed and identified in FM 22-51.

C. *Class Procedure and Lesson Tie-in.* Lecture. This lecture pertains to leaders' responsibility to identify, treat, and prevent battle fatigue. Additional subject areas pertaining to leaders' responsibilities will be discussed in subsequent classes.

II. EXPLANATION

A. *Definition of Battle Fatigue.*

    1.   Battle fatigue is a broad group of physical, mental, and emotional signs that naturally result from the heavy mental and emotional work of facing danger under difficult conditions. Its symptoms have in common that they—

        a.   Feel unpleasant.

        b.   May interfere with mission performance.

c.   Improve with reassurance, rest, replenishment of physical needs, and activities which restore confidence.

2.   Battle fatigue is the US Army's official, doctrinal term for combat stress behaviors which fit the definition given (AR 40-216).

NOTE: The term battle fatigue *is to be used whether the signs occur in a new soldier or in a veteran after months of combat. It is to be used whether the signs start before shooting starts, during the action, or in a letdown period before further action. It can occur in headquarters and CSS soldiers who are not themselves under fire but are performing demanding duties under the threat of danger or serious failure.*

3.   There are differences among the terms *battle fatigue, stressors, combat stress,* and *other combat stress behaviors.*

a.   Stressors are the causes of combat stress. They are events or situations which require a change, create internal conflict, or pose a threat. Combat stressors are any stressors which occur in the context of performing one's combat mission (whether under fire or not). For example:

(1) A 155 mm round exploding 100 meters away.

(2) Your platoon leader being wounded.

(3) Receiving a letter from wife or girlfriend which says she is going away with another man.

(4) A windchill factor of -10°F.

A stressor plus the soldier's perception of that stressor causes stress.

b.   Combat stress is the internal psychological and physiological process within the individual soldier of reacting to and dealing with the combat stressors. Stress depends much on the individual's appraisal of the stressor and its context. For example:

(1) Was that 155 mm round you heard an enemy one catching you in the open, or was it the final round of friendly protective fire just as the enemy is about to overrun you?

(2) Have the class think of examples for each of the other stressors listed above which would greatly influence the resulting stress.

Combat stress at any given time is the result of many stressors: fear of death, fear of failure, other intense painful emotions like grief and guilt, uncertainty, boredom, worries about what is happening back home, and the many physical and mental demands of combat duties. Combat stress is the cause of battle fatigue.

    c. Combat stress behaviors are the observable behaviors which the soldier shows as the result of the internal stress (either to overcome the stress, to escape it, to make it more tolerable, or to have a side effect of it). Battle fatigue is one group of combat stress behaviors. There are also other combat stress reactions.

    (1) Some are positive (like alertness, exceptional strength and endurance, loyalty to comrades, and acts of heroism).

    (2) Some are negative (like malingering, self-inflicted wounds, committing criminal acts, abusing drugs, going absent without leave, or refusing to obey orders). These others are not called battle fatigue, although battle fatigue may be present along with them if they really are reactions to combat stress. These are misconduct stress behaviors.

    (a) The misconduct may or may not interfere with specific combat tasks and may even be done by otherwise excellent soldiers, but it is harmful to discipline, is illegal, and is contrary to the UCMJ.

    (b) The misconduct stress behaviors can be prevented by good leadership, but once they occur, they require administrative action, specific medical or surgical treatment, and/or punishment. For example, malingerers must be counseled and returned to their units. Soldiers with self-inflicted wounds require line-of-duty investigations which may warrant disciplinary action. If line-of-duty is no, these soldiers may incur all cost associated with their treatment, hospitalization, and recovery. Soldiers who desert or violate the Law of Land Warfare must be punished.

    (3) Combat stress or good combat performance do not excuse criminal acts. Misconduct stress behaviors must be prevented.

    d. The difficult combat conditions (stressors) which cause battle fatigue may include sleep loss, dehydration, muscular fatigue, and such physical stressors as heat, cold, or noise. However, these are not necessarily the causes.

e. Like physical fatigue, battle fatigue can develop at either a slow or fast rate. Its speed of onset depends on the intensity and duration of the stress and on the soldier's prior training, experience, and fitness.

f. Battle fatigue usually improves when a soldier can rest and replenish himself with food, water, and sleep. It is just as important to restore his self-confidence.

g. Battle fatigue is a simple, common sense name for a natural, common condition which is not a medical or psychiatric illness.

NOTE: You may explain to the class that experience from WWI and WWII shows that soldiers tend to develop signs that are harder to manage if dramatic terms like "psych casualty" or "battle shock" are used. Fatigue is a better word than exhaustion. It applies to the mild as well as to the heavy cases and implies that the condition improves quickly.

4. The terms *stress fatigue* or *conflict fatigue* can be used for the same signs occurring under stressful conditions where no actual combat is involved. For example, stress fatigue is common among officers and NCOs at the National Training Center. All the information in this lesson can and should be used there and in garrison.

B. *Normal, Common Signs and Warning Signs of Battle Fatigue*

1. The following are facts about the normal, common signs:

a. Most soldiers have some of these signs some of the time (before, during, and after combat or danger).

b. Some soldiers have many of these signs often, yet they still fight well and perform all essential duties.

c. All soldiers, especially leaders, need to know that these are normal and common so they will not worry about them too much.

d. Key point: These signs are so normal that you should look closer at soldiers who never show any. Maybe they are just controlling their stress and fear exceedingly well. But maybe they do not realize the danger. Or, maybe the absence of the normal response is a warning sign of more serious battle fatigue.

      e.   The normal, common signs include some physical and some mental/emotional signs. Company and platoon leaders must ensure that squad and section leaders familiarize every soldier with these signs.

NOTE: Direct the class to look at page 2 of GTA 21-3-4 (Handout 1) which shows the normal, common signs. You may make transparencies if you wish. If time permits, stimulate discussion. Draw on the experience of any combat veterans or those who have taken part in highly competitive or dangerous sports or in training such as parachuting or rappelling. Make the following key points:

• Most of the physical signs are the result of having an increased amount of adrenaline in the bloodstream. These physical signs are likely to worsen when a person cannot be physically active or when he stays keyed up for a long time without resting.

• The mental signs are natural in situations where high stress, fear, or fatigue temporarily overload the brain's ability to process information. The emotional signs are likely to occur because bad things do happen in combat to cause normal grief, guilt, resentment, and doubt.

    2.   The following are facts about the warning signs:

      a.   Warning means that these are signs which deserve special attention and leadership action.

      b.   Warning signs do not necessarily mean that the soldier needs to be relieved of duty or be evacuated as a casualty. Immediate action by leaders, buddies, or the soldiers themselves may be all that is required.

      c.   Any of the normal, common signs become warning signs if they interfere with essential performance even after the soldier's buddies or leaders have taken action to help them.

      d.   Normal, common signs should be considered warning signs if they do not improve when the soldier gets a good chance to rest. However, these signs may not go away completely while the war continues. The soldier may have to learn to live with some of them. Some of the signs may even continue for a time after the soldier's return from combat to his home.

e. The signs must be considered in relation to a soldier's usual way of reacting. Take them more seriously if they come as a big change from how that soldier usually reacts to danger or interacts with other people.

NOTE: Give examples, such as the following:

• New troops being startled at the loud sound of friendly outgoing artillery is normal and common. It is a warning sign in experienced veterans.

• It is a warning when the soldier who is usually quiet turns rowdy and complains. It is a warning when the unit complainer turns quiet.

NOTE: Direct the class to page 3 of GTA 21-3-5 (Handout 2). Alternatively, you may make transparencies. Be sure that the class understands that some of the warning signs differ from the normal, common signs only in degree or the situation. Give examples such as the following:

• Fidgeting and trembling are normal and common, while constantly moving around or obvious shaking are warning signs.

• Trembling of the hands before action is normal and common, but the same trembling while performing a critical combat task is a warning sign if it may result in mission failure.

NOTE: Some of the signs are always warning signs in the sense of requiring some immediate leader action. They may be a sign of dangerous physical or mental illness. For example:

• Seeing or hearing things which aren't there is always a warning sign. It may endanger the mission or be a sign of serious illness. However, seeing things which are not there does occur often in otherwise perfectly normal people when they go a long time without sleep. They recover when they get sleep and may not necessarily have to leave the unit or get medical evaluation.

C. *Leaders' Treatment of Normal, Common Signs and Warning (More Serious) Signs of Battle Fatigue*

NOTE: This part of the lesson plan concerns what should be taught to team, section, squad, and platoon leaders about treating battle fatigue. These intervening actions for battle fatigue by junior leaders may require some soldiers to leave the small unit. These actions may require that soldiers be sent to locations where the more senior officer, NCO, or medic makes the decision pertaining to the soldiers' duty status. Company-level leaders will be familiar with treating battle fatigue and know the intervening actions they implement at their level. Company-level leaders are responsible for teaching and supervising treatment for common and warning signs of battle fatigue.

1.   What soldiers should do for self and buddy when showing signs of battle fatigue is outlined in GTA 21-3-4 (Handout 1). If time permits, familiarize the class with pages 3 and 4 or use a transparency made from that section to show what is covered. Senior leaders should ensure that junior leaders review this material with their soldiers and have them practice it regularly.

2.   Leader actions for normal, common signs (which also should be used for warning signs) are outlined in GTA 21-3-5 (Handout 2). Senior leaders should review the material with junior leaders and have them practice it regularly.

NOTE: Direct the class to pages 4 and 5 of GTA 21-3-5 (Handout 2) or use transparencies. Stimulate discussion about any techniques which may be unfamiliar. Make the following points:

• These actions are basic leadership techniques with which most of you are already familiar.
• These actions are also preventive; they reduce the combat stress

that causes battle fatigue and help soldiers cope with the normal, common signs to make them less likely to become more serious.

3. Leaders' actions for warning signs are also outlined in GTA 21-3-5 (Handout 2). This information should be reviewed with junior leaders.

a. These step-by-step actions safeguard the unit's mission and its members, get the battle-fatigued soldier to a safer place, and begin the process of restoring the soldier's confidence. (At least the actions do not undermine it further.)

b. One recommended action is to avoid taking a soldier's weapon away unless he seems so unreliable that he may use the weapon dangerously. The soldier's self-identity as a soldier who is trusted and needed by comrades is the strongest factor pulling him back from battle fatigue to effective duty. Taking his weapon away gives the message "We don't trust you" or "You are not a good soldier," unless you counteract this message by what you say when you take the weapon.

NOTE: If time permits, stimulate discussion about what might be involved to "do whatever must be done to control the soldier" in order to protect the mission and the unit. Consider different types of situations. Point out that crazy, dangerous, and violent behavior is unusual in pure battle fatigue but may occur more often in other types of combat stress behaviors, especially those involving drug abuse.

c. What leader and buddies do and say on the spot has an extremely important effect on how quickly soldiers recover and even on whether they ever recover. The right words may make extremely serious warning signs of battle fatigue get better in minutes or even seconds. Even if they do not work immediately, they help soldiers recover as quickly as possible.

4. Junior leaders' actions bring soldiers who fail to improve to the point where a more senior officer, NCO, and/or medic must make the decision whether these soldiers stay in the platoon or company or be sent elsewhere. This requires that battle fatigue cases be classified as duty, rest, or heavy. Note that duty, rest, and heavy were originally

classified as mild, moderate, and severe in the 1986 version of GTA 21-3-6. They have been changed to duty, rest, and heavy in the 1991 updates of those GTAs to conform with FM 22-51.

NOTE: Explain that the section/squad leader does not need to know how to make this classification. The first sergeant, company commander, and company medic must know it. They should teach it to the platoon leaders, platoon sergeants, and platoon medics. Direct the class to page 2 of GTA 21-3-6 (Handout 3) or use transparencies made from that page.

D. *Duty, Rest, and Heavy Battle Fatigue*

1.   Cases of battle fatigue are classified according to where they can be managed. The three classifications are outlined in GTA 21-3-6 (Handout 3) and are defined below.

a.   Duty. The soldier remains in the small unit (section or platoon) to rest and be restored to full duty.

b.   Rest. The soldier cannot remain in the small unit and must be sent to another supporting unit for temporary rest and replenishment, but not necessarily to a medical unit.

c.   Heavy. The soldier must be sent to a physician, physician assistant, or mental health officer for evaluation.

Note: Tell the class that the labels duty, rest, *and* heavy *should be thought of as nothing more than "tickets" which say where the soldier should go at this time. They are temporary triage categories (like immediate, minimal, delayed, and expectant in surgical triage). The following points (or criteria) are used to decide where the soldier can be treated.*

2.   *Duty* applies to soldiers who—

a.   Show normal, common signs, feel uncomfortable, but are 100 percent effective.

b.   Show warning signs and may be partially or even completely ineffective, but are not an unacceptable risk or burden to the unit in the tactical situation.

c.   Do not need urgent medical evaluation.

3.   *Rest* applies to soldiers who must be sent to another nonmedical unit for a period of rest.

a.   They are too much of a risk or burden to stay with their own unit at this time, given its tactical mission.

b.   The soldiers' own units cannot provide a sufficiently safe, stable environment for rest and replenishment at this time.

c.   The soldiers are not too disruptive or potentially dangerous for a unit with a less demanding mission at this time.

d.   They do not need urgent medical evaluation to rule out some possible serious physical cause or illness for the signs they are showing.

NOTE: Point out that whether a case of battle fatigue is called duty *or* rest *depends more on the tactical situation, mission, and resources of the small unit than it does on the signs the soldier is showing. A unit which is just being pulled back into reserve can keep a soldier who might have to be left behind if the unit were just leaving for action behind enemy lines. Use examples from your type of unit.*

4.   *Heavy* applies to any soldier with more serious warning signs who fits within one or both of the categories below.

a.   The soldier is too burdensome, disruptive, or possibly dangerous to keep in the small unit or in any available nonmedical support unit at this time.

b.   The soldier's symptoms could be due to a physical cause which may need urgent medical/surgical treatment (for example, head or spine injury, drug abuse).

NOTE: Heavy *is now being used instead of* severe *because too many people kept confusing* severe *with the more serious signs and reading into the word more negative meaning than it deserves. The difference between* rest *and* heavy *is influenced more by the kind of signs the soldier is showing than was the difference between* duty *and* rest, *although the availability of other CSS units can still affect this classification.*

NOTE: Once the soldier reaches the medical system, they subdivide
heavy *into* refer *(meaning send to the next echelon medical facility for*
evaluation) and hold *(meaning hold for treatment at this medical*
facility). However, there is no need to explain this distinction to non-
medical audiences since it applies only after the soldier has arrived and
has been evaluated by the physician or physician assistant.

5.   There is no easy rule for deciding whether a warning sign
makes the soldier a case of duty, rest, or heavy battle fatigue. That will
require judgment based on what the leader and, perhaps, the unit
medic know about the individual soldier: what has happened to the
soldier; how the soldier responds to helping actions; what is likely to
happen to the unit next; and what resources are available to the unit.
Any warning sign that can be listed in a few words may be duty battle fatigue in one case, be rest in another, and be heavy in a third case.

6.   Signs which would usually cause the case to be sorted as
heavy include the following:

a.   Dangerous, threatening behavior which is not just a disciplinary problem.

b.   Hallucinations and delusions not explained by sleep loss.

c.   Serious memory loss.

d.   Extreme pain.

e.   Loss of a major physical function, such as vision or the
ability to move an arm.

f.   Complete unresponsiveness; not moving or answering at
all.

NOTE: Any of these cases might still be classified as rest or even as duty
if the signs occur in response to extreme stress and clear up quickly.

7.   The heavy classification does not necessarily mean that a soldier is less likely to recover or will take longer to recover than cases
classified as duty or rest.

8.   Company leaders' actions for duty and rest battle-fatigued

soldiers are outlined in GTA 21-3-6 (Handout 3). Company commanders, first sergeants, and company medics should know and practice them and teach them to platoon-level leaders and medics.

NOTE: Direct the class to Handout 3, page 2, or use transparencies made from pages 2 and 3, or briefly discuss the list. You should adapt these recommendations to your unit. Stimulate discussion on how it needs to be adapted. For example:

• The supporting units where soldiers can be rested will be different for maneuver companies in an armor or a light infantry battalion, for an artillery battery, for a dispersed corps-level signal company, or for a maintenance or a transportation company.

• Options include resting the soldier in another platoon of your company; in another line company in the battalion; or at the battalion headquarters and headquarters company in the field trains.

• Some small detachments may not have first sergeants or platoon/company/battalion organization. They may be attached to other units for support. Determine where to rest battle-fatigued soldiers in your situation.

9. The following are key points:

a. The first sergeant or NCOIC has to take the soldiers and find them a safer, quieter place to rest and work for a day or two. Note that instructions for the leader of the unit who receives the soldiers temporarily are included in GTA 21-3-5, page 6.

b. If the soldier's small unit cannot wait for the first sergeant/NCOIC to take the soldier, it may be necessary to evacuate to the supporting medical element. If so, every effort should be made there to remove the soldier from medical channels to a nonmedical unit for further rest, replenishment, and reassurance.

c. A first sergeant/NCOIC who cannot find a suitable support unit can try to arrange a place to sleep at a medical unit which has empty cots. This alternative is not preferred, and the soldier must understand he is not a patient, just a tired soldier.

d. The soldier must remain accounted for and not get lost in the shuffle. There must be a positive plan to return the soldier to the original unit in a short time, and the soldier must know this.

e.   Every reasonable effort should be made to maintain personal contact between the soldier and the original unit.

10.   Leader actions for *heavy* battle-fatigued soldiers are the same as for the *rest* battle-fatigued except that the soldiers are evacuated medically, as soon as possible, to be examined by a physician or physician assistant.

a.   They may be successfully treated and released within hours (as *duty* or *rest* battle fatigue), or may be held there for rest and treatment for a day or two, or may be evacuated further to the rear. What happens depends on their signs and the medical unit's situation.

b.   If treated close to their units, 50 to 85 percent (average: 75 percent) of heavy battle fatigue casualties return to duty within 1 to 3 days. About 15 to 20 percent more may return to other duty (usually in other units) in 1 to 2 weeks. Only 5 to 10 percent have to be evacuated home, and they usually have other problems besides battle fatigue.

c.   However, if evacuated too far too fast, few battle-fatigued soldiers return to duty. Many may remain permanently disabled.

11.   Recovered battle-fatigued soldiers who return to their units and are welcomed there do not have a higher rate of battle fatigue than other soldiers. They are less likely to break again (or to be killed or wounded) than is a new replacement who is a stranger in the unit.

NOTE: Emphasize to the class that a good soldier will be good again. A new soldier who becomes a battle fatigue casualty deserves another chance. Being new to combat and a stranger in the unit are two high-stress/high-risk factors. These factors have been partially overcome if that soldier returns to the same unit and is welcomed there. But also emphasize the following point and stimulate discussion on how it should be handled.

12.   Someone who has always been a poor soldier is not going to be made into a good one simply by treatment for battle fatigue. The soldier may need to be reassigned to some other job or unit (or be discharged as unsuitable).

E. *Basic Principles of Preventing Battle Fatigue*

1.   While the average ratio of battle fatigue casualties to wounded in action is one for every three to five, elite units consistently have fewer than one for ten wounded. We cannot prevent battle fatigue in highly stressful combat; however, we can prevent battle fatigue casualties who require treatment in the medical system.

2.   GTA 21-3-6 (Handout 3) shows factors that increase battle fatigue casualties and leaders' actions to prevent them. These should be taught by battalion and company leaders to their platoon leaders.

3.   The following are key principles for reducing the stress of combat and preventing battle fatigue casualties:

a.   Encourage unit cohesion by integrating new replacements quickly, assigning buddies, and using other team-building techniques. Unit cohesion is the personal trust and loyalty of soldiers who have worked together to overcome hardship and danger to achieve a common objective.

b.   Stabilize the home front by helping soldiers resolve their home front problems. An Israeli study found that having uncertainties at home was the strongest factor which distinguished soldiers who became stress casualties from those who were decorated for valor. Unit cohesion was second strongest.

c.   Instill unit pride by honoring historical examples of initiative, endurance and resilience, of overcoming heavy odds, and of self-sacrifice leading to triumph. This is needed to give direction and hope to the cohesive unit so that it does not become preoccupied solely with the survival and comfort of its members.

d.   Assure physical fitness. This must enhance muscle strength and agility as well as endurance through a regular training program. Not being physically fit almost guarantees battle fatigue when the going gets rough.

e.   Conduct tough, realistic training that is as much like the combat mission and environment as possible (sights, sounds, pace, confusion, fatigue, discomfort, and feedback). Soldiers' first exposure to combat, to enemy weapons and tactics, and to strange, hostile climates produces battle fatigue.

f.   Practice casualty care and evacuation routinely. Everyone must know lifesaving techniques for self and buddy. Talk about the possible loss of leaders and comrades. Prepare junior leaders (and yourself) to take over. This way soldiers know that they can receive immediate care and the chain of command will not break.

g. Plan and practice sleep discipline. Plan ahead to make sure all soldiers get enough sleep, especially leaders and those with critical tasks. Sleep discipline means reviewing sleep as a resource to allocate to soldiers just like water, food, ammunition, and fuel.

III. SUMMARY

A. When in combat, you, the leader, must try to conserve the soldiers' strength and well-being with food, water, shelter, hygiene, medical care, and rest. In contrast to the training situation, you do not deliberately seek hardship. When you must accept it because of circumstances or better accomplishment of the mission, you will explain the reasons to the troops. And, because you have trained hard together, you can remind the soldiers of how all of you suffered in training and still accomplished the mission just to prepare for this kind of combat situation.

B. Use the three handouts. They are available at the local US Army Training and Audiovisual Support Center. They are intended for leaders to use as aids in opportunity training for their subordinates during field exercises. They will also serve as a reminder (checklist) in mobilization and combat.

1. GTA 21-3-4 (Battle Fatigue, Normal, Common Signs, What to do for Self and Buddy) is intended for all soldiers, especially the junior enlisted.

2. GTA 21-3-5 (Battle Fatigue, "More Serious" Signs: Leader Actions) is intended for all leaders, especially those at team, squad, section, and platoon level.

3. GTA 21-3-6 (Battle Fatigue, Company Leader Actions and Prevention) is intended for platoon leaders and above.

ABBREVIATIONS AND ACRONYMS

AIDS	acquired immunodeficiency syndrome	CONOPS	continuous operations
AMEDDC&S	Army Medical Department Center and School	CONUS	continental United States
		CSS	combat service support
AR	Army Regulation	DA	Department of the Army
attn	attention		
AWOL	absent without leave	DNBI	disease and non-battle injuries
BAS	battalion aid station	DOW	died of wounds
		DSM III-R	*Diagnostic and Statistical Manual of Mental Disorders,* Third Edition, Revised
C4I	command, control, communications, computers and intelligence		
CAARNG	California Army National Guard	EPW	enemy prisoner(s) of war
CIP	Command Information Program	FID	Foreign Internal Defense
COHORT	cohesion, operational readiness training	FM	field manual
		G1	Assistant Chief of Staff (Personnel)
COMMZ	communications zone	G2	Assistant Chief of Staff (Intelligence)

G3	Assistant Chief of Staff (Operations and Plans)	PTSD	post-traumatic stress disorder
G4	Assistant Chief of Staff (Logistics)	PW	prisoner(s) of war
G5	Assistant Chief of Staff (Civil Affairs)	R&R	rest and recuperation
GTA	Graphic Training Aid	S1	Adjutant
		S2	Intelligence Officer
HN	host nation	S3	Operations and Training Officer
IDAD	Internal Defense and Development	S4	Supply Officer
KIA	killed in action	S5	Civil Affairs Officer
MIA	missing in action	SOF	special operations forces
MOPP	mission-oriented protective posture	SPRINT	Special Psychiatric Rapid Intervention Team
MRE	meal(s), ready to eat	STD	sexually transmitted diseases
NBC	nuclear, biological, and chemical	SUSOPS	sustained operations
NCA	national command authority	TOE	table of organization and equipment
NCO	noncommissioned officer	TSOP	tactical standing operating procedure
NCOIC	noncommissioned officer in charge		
NEO	noncombatant evacuation operation	UCMJ	Uniform Code of Military Justice
		US	United States
NYDN	not yet diagnosed, nervous	WIA	wounded in action
		WWI	World War I
PSYOP	psychological operations	WWII	World War II

REFERENCES

SOURCES USED

These are the sources quoted or paraphrased in this publication.

Army Publications

AR 310-25. *Dictionary of United States Army Terms (Short Title: AD).* 15 October 1983. (Reprinted with basic including Change 1, May 1986.)

AR 310-50. *Authorized Abbreviations, Brevity Codes, and Acronyms.* 15 November 1985.

DA Pamphlet 25-37. *Index of Graphic Training Aids (GTA).* 1 July 1991.

FM 12-50. *US Army Bands.* 6 September 1991.

FM 16-1. *Religious Support Doctrine: The Chaplain and Chaplain Assistant.* 27 November 1989.

FM 22-5. *Drill and Ceremonies.* 8 December 1986.

FM 22-102. *Soldier Team Development.* 2 March 1987.

FM 100-2-1. *Soviet Army Operations and Tactics.* 16 July 1984.

FM 100-37. *Terrorism Counteraction.* 24 July 1987.

DOCUMENTS NEEDED

These documents must be available to the intended users of this publication.

Multiservice Publications

FM 100-20. *Military Operations in Low Intensity Conflict.* AFP 3-20. 5 December 1990.

Army Publications

AR 40-216.	*Neuropsychiatry and Mental Health.* 10 August 1984.
*AR 165-1.	*Chaplain Activities in the United States Army.* 31 August 1989.
*FM 8-42.	*Medical Operations in Low Intensity Conflict.* 4 December 1990.
FM 21-20.	*Physical Fitness Training.* 28 August 1985.
*FM 22-9.	*Soldier Performance in Continuous Operations.* 8 December 1983.
*FM 22-100.	*Military Leadership.* 31 July 1990.
FM 25-101.	*Battle Focused Training.* 30 September 1990.
*FM 90-10.	*Military Operations on Urbanized Terrain (MOUT) (How to Fight).* 15 August 1979.
*FM 90-10-1.	*An Infantryman's Guide to Urban Combat (How to Fight).* 15 August 1979.
*FM 100-5.	*Operations.* 5 May 1986.
GTA 21-3-4.	*Battle Fatigue, Normal, Common Signs, What to do for Self and Buddy.* June 1986.
GTA 21-3-5.	*Battle Fatigue, "More Serious" Signs: Leader Actions.* June 1986.
GTA 21-3-6.	*Battle Fatigue, Company Leader Actions and Prevention.* June 1986.

Nonmilitary Publications

American Psychiatric Association. *Diagnostic and Statistical Manual of Mental Disorders.* Third Edition, Revised. Washington, D.C.: American Psychiatric Association, 1987.

READINGS RECOMMENDED

These readings contain relevant supplemental information.

Army Publications

DA Pamphlet 600-63-10.
   Stress Management Module for "Fit to Win" Program. September 1987.

*This source was also used to develop this publication.

FM 8-10-4.

Medical Platoon Leaders' Handbook. 16 November 1990.

Mullins, W.S. and Glass, H.A., eds.

The Medical Department of the US Army, Neuropsychiatry in World War II (1973). Overseas Theaters, OTSG, Department of the Army Washington, D.C.

The Medical Department of the US Army in The World War 10 (1920). Neuropsychiatry, War Department, Washington, D.C.

Summers, Harry G. Jr. *On Strategy, The Vietnam War in Context.* Carlisle Barracks, Pennsylvania: US Army War Department, 1981.

Nonmilitary Publications

Cable, Larry. *Conflict of Myths: The Development of American Counterinsurgency Doctrine and the Vietnam War.* New York: New York University Press, 1986.

Belenky, Gregory, ed. *Contemporary Studies in Combat Psychiatry.* New York: Greenwood Press, 1987.

Du Picq, Ardant. *Battle Studies,* trans. John N. Greely and Robert C. Cotton. (Harrisburg: Military: Military Service Publishing Company, 1947.)

Fanon, Frantz. *The Wretched of the Earth.* New York: Grove Press, First Evergreen Black Cat Edition, 1968.

Gifford, R.K. and Tyler, M.P. "Consulting in Grief Leadership—A Practical Guide." *Disaster Management 2,* No. 4 (1990).

Holmes, Richard. *Acts of War: Behaviors of Men in Combat.* New York: Free Press, 1985.

Horne, Alistair. *A Savage War of Peace.* New York: Viking Press, 1978.

Kellet, Anthony. *Combat Motivation: The Behavior of Soldiers in Battle.* Boston: Kluer-Nijhoff, 1982.

Marshall, S.L.A. *Bringing Up the Rear.* Presidio Press, 1979.

Swank, Roy L., and Marchand, Walter E. "Combat Neurosis." *Archives of Neurology 55* (1946): 236-46.

INDEX

U.S. ARMY
COMBAT
STRESS
CONTROL
HANDBOOK

—